The Secret of Life

A Manual for Total Self Worth And a Brilliant Future

by

Paul Upchurch

AF472768

TRAFFORD
USA ▪ Canada ▪ UK ▪ Ireland

© Copyright 2005 Paul Upchurch.
All rights reserved. No part of this publication may be reproduced, stored in a retrieval system, or transmitted, in any form or by any means, electronic, mechanical, photocopying, recording, or otherwise, without the written prior permission of the author.

Note for Librarians: a cataloguing record for this book that includes Dewey Decimal Classification and US Library of Congress numbers is available from the Library and Archives of Canada. The complete cataloguing record can be obtained from their online database at:
www.collectionscanada.ca/amicus/index-e.html
ISBN 1-4120-4963-6

TRAFFORD

Offices in Canada, USA, Ireland, UK and Spain
This book was published on-demand in cooperation with Trafford Publishing. On-demand publishing is a unique process and service of making a book available for retail sale to the public taking advantage of on-demand manufacturing and Internet marketing. On-demand publishing includes promotions, retail sales, manufacturing, order fulfilment, accounting and collecting royalties on behalf of the author.
Book sales for North America and international:
Trafford Publishing, 6E-2333 Government St.,
Victoria, BC V8T 4P4 CANADA
phone 250 383 6864 (toll-free 1 888 232 4444)
fax 250 383 6804; email to orders@trafford.com
Book sales in Europe:
Trafford Publishing (UK) Ltd., Enterprise House, Wistaston Road Business Centre,
Wistaston Road, Crewe, Cheshire CW2 7RP UNITED KINGDOM
phone 01270 251 396 (local rate 0845 230 9601)
facsimile 01270 254 983; orders.uk@trafford.com
Order online at:
www.trafford.com/robots/04-2771.html

10 9 8 7 6 5 4 3

The phrase "Blue Sky" in business means the potential for unlimited revenue from any given venture. I have put a "Blue Sky" on this cover to represent the unlimited potential for your life that I want you to realize from the reading of this book.

The cover is an actual photo taken by staff photographer Mike Valeri for his newspaper in Massachusetts, USA. Can you see the Angel in the cloud? Remember this is an untouched, actual photo taken for a newspaper. Nobody knew the Angel was there until a reader noticed it. It's amazing!

So, not only is the cover a "Blue Sky" but there is also an Angel there watching over and protecting you while you read this book.

ACKNOWLEDGMENTS

FIRSTLY I WANT TO THANK MY WIFE Tracey Boyd who has supported me fantastically in regards to, not only this book, but my entire life's journey I've had with her. Also my three beautiful children, Miller, Gus and Bessi. They are my Angels! I want to thank Bernard McInerney and Karina Godwin who have also supported me with this book and are two of the most generous and loving friends a person could have.

I would also like to thank my very large family for teaching me about love and about how to have fun in life! Many thanks to my two "best mates" since high school, Chris Baker and Robert Spencer. You guys have taught me about loyalty, love and the true meaning of friendship. Also to Wilma and Neville Lambert who have also supported me in my life and who taught me, by example, all about unconditional love, selflessness, generosity of spirit and a love for the written word.

Thank you to Mike Valeri who let me use his wonderful photo as my cover, and to Douglas Davies who first alerted me to the photo.

Special thanks to my good friend Kim Trengove. She performed editing work on the book. You're a gem Kim.

If I've left anyone out, let me know and I'll put you in the next book!

Finally I'd like to thank my dearly departed mum and dad, Miller snr and Emily Upchurch, for raising me with respect, love, warmth and, most importantly, humour. Dad showed me that it's possible to live life as a good man whilst being true to oneself. Mum showed me how important it is to love the children. Thank you, you two. I miss you still. Always will.

Cheers,
Paul

Part One

Everything You Need To Know About You And Your World

INDEX

It's a funny thing about life;
If you refuse to accept,
Anything but the best,
You very often get it

W. SOMERSET MAUGHAM

OK, SO, ARE YOU READY? Are you ready to finally take control of your life? No more mucking around and faking it. No more pretending that "I'm doing fine thank you very much". No, this is for real my friend. Are you seriously ready to take control and heal your life and move forward towards a happier, prosperous, abundant, loving and fulfilling future? If you're not then put this book down right now! Only ever pick it up again when you *really know* you're ready because it's going to take some work. Work and commitment. You have to know, deep, deep down, that your life-long and everlasting happiness is actually worth putting in the hard yards for. You have to know that you're truly worthy of having everything you ever thought you could have. That your dreams can really come true and that you are the person who can make them come true.

I think you're ready. In fact, I know it. The mere fact that you've read this far means you're willing to do some work towards the future you've always known you could live. So keep reading and don't be frightened. It's going to be fun and we're going to be concentrating on the best subject in the world... .you! All I ask is that you don't ever let yourself be sidetracked from your purpose once you begin the path that is set down for you throughout this book. Your lack of self worth, (and we all have a degree of a lack of self worth even if we're not aware of it), and your negative thoughts from deep in your subconscious will attempt to steer you off the path. Your subconscious doesn't like change. Even change for the good! So even if you try to change your life for the better, your subconscious will try to sabotage it in the beginning. Don't let this happen! Use discipline, vigilance and persistence to see you through.

I'm going to give you all the information you're ever going to need in order to heal your life and move on positively to that bright, stress-free future. After that I'll break down, chapter by chapter, many of the facets, issues and conditions of life that affect us in our life's journey and give you affirmations, healing techniques, meditations and visualizations that relate to each specific issue or topic.

I have found, through healings, research and a lot of life experience, that virtually everybody's issues, whether they are concerning work, family, themselves, illness, relationships, or the lack-of-relationships, all come down to one basic and simple cause**. That cause is a palpable lack of self-worth or self-love. Not enough self-love**. It's at the root of all our problems I promise you. From being unable to make decisions to being unable to accept love and intimacy to real physical problems to major illness. All of these "conditions" or "issues" have a depth of a lack of self-worth/self-love as their root cause. In this book, you're going to discover the reasons for this lack and learn the tools to make the changes required to instill self-love back into your life and change your life for the better...forever.

True unconditional self-love, without ego attached, is the state we're after.

This is Enlightenment. This is the true path. The true journey. I know this is an easy thing to say and a much harder thing to do. But you have to always remember that your happiness and well being is absolutely worth the work. You'll find that when you achieve this state of true unconditional self-love it will feel as if a bright white light shines out from inside of you for all the world to see. Everything and everyone you have ever wanted can come and will come to you then. You will be magnetic.

But remember this is all without ego being involved. If the ego gets in there, even for a second, it can ruin the process. When we let ego in we know we're stuck in this world's petty issues that promote judgment of self and of others and we don't want to do that. We've got to beware of the ego. Our ego's are pretty slippery little devils and take some watching in order for us to be in control. For instance, if you ever experience jealousy, then that's your ego at work. If you judge others, that's your ego at work. If you blame others for your state of affairs, if you're hurt by what others may say, if you rely too much on positive reinforcement, then this is all just your ego working overtime.

A state of true self-love, without ego, means you're in a constant, even state of happiness. Not too much and not too little. All the dramatic highs and lows are removed from your life. You're not dependent on whether people are nice or nasty to you. That type of reinforcement has no effect on you any longer. If you know and love yourself, without ego, then you know how wonderful you truly are and compliments will only reinforce that for you. You won't depend on compliments for your well-being. By the same token insults won't affect you as you will have taken complete responsibility for all your actions and will have nothing to hide. You will understand that for someone to insult another then they must be in a sate of a lack of self-love and are blaming others for whatever it is they are lacking in their lives at that moment.

True self-love exists without judgment. It means being totally responsible for all ones own actions and allowing others to be responsible for theirs. It's a totally liberating state to be in.

It takes a lot of work on your part to make significant change in your life. Remember, though, that this is the very best work you'll ever have to do in your life. You will be putting in overtime without penalty rates. Your rewards won't be monetary, they'll be a whole new life. Gee, a good bargain I think! But it does have to be you that does the work. There is no magic wand that you can find to use. You won't be able to sit on your bum and wait for a guru or guru-ess to come along and change your life for you. That's just not going to happen and you'll end up wasting half your life expecting a miracle to happen (and you'll get a really, really fat bum).

"If I read ALL the self-help books then my life will change"! "If I go to ALL the wonderful new-age courses then my life will change"! No it won't! All the self-help books and all the new-age courses in the world won't change your life in a positive way unless you are willing to change and are willing to put in the work needed to make that change happen and then remain with you permanently.

Going on living your life with the same old patterns will do nothing but reproduce the same old outcomes. Nothing will change. In fact the first sign of insanity is repeating the same actions over and over again but expecting different outcomes. That's just crazy folks. We've got to put in new stimuli to achieve new results.

It also takes vigilance, discipline and persistence to make serious, positive change work in your life. You need trust and patience. I don't want to scare you off here. Believe me, these are all things that you can do. Part of the process of building your self-esteem is allowing yourself to believe that you are capable.

You are the guru! It all comes from you. Don't look without for all the answers. They aren't out there. You only have to look within and find them all. Yes the books and courses will help. There will be messages and signs in all of them for you. You only need to seek and find the information that resonates with you and take it and use it. But what all that information will do is trigger knowledge, belief and intuition inside of you. It will unlock previously impregnable doors of knowledge and understanding within you. It's already there. You're just not acknowledging it. For whatever reason.

What we want to do is find out why those padlocks are on, remove them, and then watch you burst out of your self imposed cocoon as a totally empowered, beautiful, successful and brilliant butterfly! Everything you'll ever need in this life is already within you. All of your power, your creativeness, your intellect, your intuition, your love, your strength, your compassion, your humility, your forgiveness, your understanding, your belief, your sexuality, your sensuality, your passion. It's all in you. You are the guru! You are the power! It's all up to you!

The information and guidance needed for your transformation is everywhere. All you have to do is to decide to look for it. The challenge is to find enough self-love to decide that you are worthy of putting all the work in to make positive change in your life.

As I've already said I'm going to structure this book by having a general discussion right now, in part one, about healing, affirmations and meditations and much more. I'm going to offer up all the tools you'll ever need to restart your life in a positive, confident and happy way. Then, in part two, I'll go through issues, one by one, that need work and I'll put specific healing, affirmations and meditations at the end of each issue for you to use in relation to that particular issue. So, sit back, get comfy, and set off on the most important journey of your life...the journey to your new life. Good luck my friend.

I am content to follow to its source,
Every event in action or in thought;
Measure the lot; forgive myself the lot!
When such as I cast out remorse,
So great a sweetness flows into the breast,
We must laugh and we must sing,
We are blest by everything,
Everything we look upon is blessed.

W.B.YEATS

THE SECRET OF LIFE

THE SECRET OF LIFE IS BASICALLY THIS: "**You can't love someone else until you love yourself**". This is an oldie but a goodie and it's probably one of the most perfect truths you will ever hear. It's inescapable. Until we truly love ourselves, unconditionally, we'll always be looking for love from others instead of looking TO love others and receive love in return. On the surface that would seem to be a subtle difference in intention. However, in reality, there is a chasm of difference in needing to be loved and in giving love in order to receive love.

We will always be carrying baggage into a relationship with another person unless we truly love and care for ourselves. We will always be projecting our own issues and problems onto our partners. If we have self-love however then we've most certainly dealt with our issues so there's nothing to project, blame or otherwise. So we never enter into a relationship with an agenda. We enter into a relationship because we know who we are and what we want. Our partner sees that and is naturally drawn to it. Ideally we have an equality within the relationship. Not one of the partners is needy of the other. They have merely been drawn together to share a beautiful and unencumbered love.

This is true for all relationships. Whether they be with a significant other, as above, or with a family member, a friend, work-mates, team-mates and so-on. Living in a state of unconditional self-love allows us to be totally free of all the previously debilitating and limiting prejudices and problems that had blocked our ability to love without a cost. People can tell when someone has a sufficient dose of self-love. They're drawn to that person because they know that entering into a relationship with that person, whether that be a romantic or platonic relationship, will not be an expensive one. Emotionally or otherwise.

Taking the time to find our unconditional self-love doesn't mean we're being selfish either. A person who is living in a state of unconditional self-love will positively affect everyone they come into contact with. That most certainly includes a significant other. Unconditional self-love acts like a magnet. People are attracted to the power, the openness, the freedom and the honesty that exudes from a person in this state. Taking the time to find your total and unconditional self-love is the most UN-selfish thing you could do!

This really is the "secret of life". It's what we're all searching for. It's what we look for in material possessions, organized religions, sporting clubs, nationalities. **The secret of life is not to look outwardly for true happiness and love but to look within**. I know it seems a rather glib thing to say on the surface. But that's just it, it's only glib on the surface. Underneath the surface is where all the action is! That's where all the real decisions are made. We need to get in there and alter the destructive patterns. We need to replace them with positive and constructive patterns of self-love and self-belief.

When we attain a state of complete unconditional self-love, without ego attached, then we have discovered the secret of life and everything and everyone we ever wanted will come into our lives. This is enlightenment. This is the way. This is the path, and just to be on the path, just to be doing the work to replace the old patterns, just to be working on loving ones-self unconditionally will change our world for the better. Validations that you're on the right path will come into your life on a daily basis in the shape of "signs". These "signs" may simply be others changing their attitudes, in a positive way, towards you. They may also include hearing pertinent songs on the radio, characters from films and television shows and such saying just the things you need to hear at that moment in time. Good things will happen. Be aware and keep your eye out for the signs of validation telling you you're on the right track. They will be there.

It's also very important to enjoy the journey. The journey is everything. For when we reach the end then we're complete and we won't have any further lives to live in order to attain enlightenment. We can then return to the source and become light. Pure, free, blissful light. This journey may take a long, long time. So, again, it's crucial to live in the moment, in the present, and to be happy in the "here and now". True self-love helps us to live this way and by living this way we help ourselves attain true self-love. It's the old "Catch 22" syndrome all over again. Except this is a very positive "Catch 22". It's "win, win" all the way. It's all love which is a very, very good thing.

Love is
Letting go of fear
GERALD JAMPOLSKY

WHAT IS LOVE?

"WHAT IS LOVE"? True love is the feelings and emotions we have when we totally, unconditionally, without judgment and ego, consider ourselves to be absolutely worthy of complete happiness. All else is just attachment for one reason or another. Some people can go through many lives being attached to many people without ever knowing true love.

We always love that new car, house, toy or whatever "thing" was just given to us or we bought for ourselves. We will love it because it says to us that someone else, or ourselves, considers us worthy of this new "thing". So it gives us enormous happiness. For a short period of time because, eventually, we'll grow out of whatever it is, it'll break, or we'll end up trading it in, selling it or throwing it out. Gone. Where's our happiness now? We loved that "thing"! The problem is that all "things" are impermanent. They don't last.

The above analogy can be applied to relationships as well. That's what is meant by "attachment" as opposed to true love.

Depending on our state of being, of where we are in our development of self-love, we can be attracted to another person for all the wrong reasons. We may see it as love but it is merely "attachment" because for whatever reason the relationship fills some gap or other in our lives at that time. But it won't last. As with the "things" just mentioned the relationship will breakdown or we'll throw it out or trade it in. Remember: **You can't love someone else until you learn to love yourself!** Never forget that statement. Never have truer words been spoken. Knowing and truly understanding that phrase will change your life, for the better, forever.

The only lasting happiness is true, unconditional self-love and the funny thing is when you are in a state of unconditional self-love you can have all the things you want. They will come and go as they're needed in your life without you even blinking an eye-lid because you will not have a need for them. You won't be dependent on them for your happiness. They will merely complement your life.

Only with true, unconditional self-love will you find someone to love forever and have them love you too, unconditionally. That is what love is.

What we are today
Comes from our thoughts of yesterday,
And our present thoughts,
Build our life of tomorrow:
Our life is the creation of our mind

THE BUDDHA

HEALING

WHAT IS HEALING? Is it like going to the doctor? Or the witch doctor? These are perfectly understandable questions and ones that I'll attempt to answer properly here. Healing people has been going on for thousands of years in many cultures and societies. In our western society healing has been a concept mostly utilized by the medical profession. However these days it's a much, much broader and sometimes subtle concept. When you're stressed, eating some food that made you feel comforted when your mum made it when you were a kid can be a form of healing. Also visiting a Kineseologist, a Reiki practitioner, a clairvoyant healer, a Sekhem practitioner, and a homeopath or naturopath are all fantastic ways to have healing. Healing is basically identifying that there is an issue that is causing your mind or body or spirit, (or all three), distress and then finding the best way, for you, to deal with that issue so that you can move on in your life in peace and comfort. You can do it by yourself also. In fact we must heal ourselves in this life if we want to divest ourselves of the debilitating negative input from the past and be able to move on positively into the future. We all have this negative input that's basically all the so-called "baggage" we carry around every single day. We've got to get rid of it. It's wearing us out. It's getting us down and stopping us from moving on to a wonderful and glorious future. The only way to get rid of it is to heal it out. Throughout this book I will offer you many ways to heal many issues and conditions as we go along. First we have to identify what those issues and conditions actually are. It's all a very nurturing, comforting and liberating process.

In fact this very process of identification and healing is as important, if not more important, than any trip to a doctor, Physiotherapist, Psychotherapist etc. We need to take care of and nurture our sub-conscious and "spiritual" selves as well as our physical selves. In fact the two are mutually inclusive. That is, you can't have one without the other.

Going down a healing path is also a major step in terms of self-worth. We must feel worthy to be healed to actually allow ourselves healing. A lot of people, believe it or not, do not deem themselves worthy of being healed and will go through life suffering debilitating conditions and states of mind with negative attitudes towards themselves that force them to live unhappy and unfulfilled lives. This is a totally unacceptable and unnecessary state of affairs

Many so called experts put down all this healing as "New-Age mumbo-jumbo". This is largely due to ignorance. People always tend to fear and therefore put down the things they don't understand. Even the term "New-Age" is totally misleading and is only used by "experts" in a denigrating fashion in order to discredit anything that threatens their status-quo. The funny thing is that most of the "New-Age" healing practices on offer at the moment have been around far longer than medical science or science in general. In fact the sciences are now not only acknowledging alternative healing practices but, in many instances, incorporating them in their own healing methodologies.

Spirituality will be mentioned throughout this book and, in my view, means an understanding and acceptance of the "greater-consciousness" and does not have any religious connotation whatsoever. The "greater-consciousness" is simply the mass conveyor of thoughts and consciousness across worlds. It explains phenomenon such as synchronicity. For instance, when you think of someone and suddenly they call you on the phone, that's called synchronicity and happens because you put the thought of that person out there into the greater-consciousness and they received it and therefore got the urge to call you.

Another example of the greater consciousness at work is the well-documented study of two separate groups of monkeys on two separate islands in the Pacific Ocean. A monkey from the group of monkeys on the first island couldn't open a coconut with his rock. He smashed and smashed the rock onto the coconut but the rock was blunt and had little effect. One day, by accident, he found that if he rubbed his little rock on the bigger rocks it created a sharp edge on his little smashing rock. When he used that sharp edge on his coconut he was able to split open his coconut successfully. The other monkeys around him began to copy this behavior and pretty soon all of the monkeys from that group on that first island began opening their coconuts with sharpened rocks. After a short period of time a group of monkeys from a separate island hundreds and hundreds of miles away also picked up a rock and began to sharpen it and use it to split open their own coconuts.

Now, it was absolutely impossible for any physical or vocal contact between the two islands. It was impossible for there to be any contact between to two groups of monkeys in any way shape or form. The notion of using the sharp rock as a new tool simply went up into the greater-consciousness and across to the other set of monkeys. This is a well-documented occurrence.

Also I'm sure you've had or know someone who has had the experience of coming up with a new idea about something, then not doing anything about it, only to see someone else do the thing they originally thought of. I know it happens to me all the time. I'm a real "ideas" type of person and it happens to me constantly. I can't go through with every idea I have. I just don't have the time or the energy, but every time I have a new idea and don't do something about it, someone else always does. Every single time! Greater-consciousness. It's real. It's how prayer works. The American Indians have always understood it and used it in their chanting.

So, spirituality and the greater consciousness are intrinsic tools used in healing and will be referred to a lot in this book in those terms. We tap into the greater consciousness when we meditate as well. That will be explained in more detail in the chapter on meditation.

To forgive,
Is to be free

PAUL UPCHURCH

FORGIVENESS

NOTHING WILL CHANGE IN YOUR WORLD and you will not move on from the negativity of the past unless you find forgiveness for all those who have transgressed against you. Holding onto hate, the need for revenge, the holding of grudges, only hurts you. It never affects the people who hurt you in the first place. They go on with their lives oblivious of the hurt inside of you. So what good is hating them? It only churns you up. It only makes you sick. It only holds you back from a positive and wonderful future.

What you must do is forgive them to liberate you in order for you to move on. It doesn't mean you forget. We make mistakes in this life. That's how we learn. So we don't forget, but we must forgive. It's crucial.

Let's say, for example, a personal friend rips you off in a business deal and puts you in debt and on the verge of bankruptcy. What you would need to do in this situation is forgive that friend for the sake of your future. Knowing that they won't be involved in that future. They forfeited the right to be your friend and you will, obviously, never be in business with them ever again. But you won't be walking around with a crippling and sickening grudge that will hurt only you.

So you've learnt your lesson, you've forgiven them and you've moved on to a brighter and wiser future.

Forgiveness is very, very powerful. It can remove deep hurt, hate, and guilt from you. It will set you free.

(There are many brilliant healers out there that can also assist in this healing process. Check local papers, magazines or simply put out a thought into the greater-consciousness and ask for a healer and one will be presented for you. Trust me this works.)

Now what we're going to do is to replace that conditioned negative dialogue with a positive one through the power of affirmations.

As you think,
So shall you be.

UNKNOWN

AFFIRMATIONS

WHAT ARE AFFIRMATIONS? A lot of people pooh-pooh affirmations as sissy, girlie, positive thinking hippy-crap! I'm just glad I don't live in the head of people who say that! They would have had a very negative upbringing and conditioning to be that defensive about anything as positive as affirmations. Obviously they are wrong in what they say. Affirmations are simply positive input to create a better life for yourself. There is no down-side in that.

Basically every second of every minute of every day in our lives we have a negative dialogue going on from our sub-conscious mind to our conscious mind. This dialogue affects everything we do and say in our lives. It affects our today and our tomorrow, our future. Affirmations are all about replacing that negative dialogue with positive dialogue. Why wouldn't we do that if we had the choice? Why wouldn't we rather be positive than negative? Be happy instead of sad? Successful instead of unsuccessful? Well the tools are now in your hands. You have the power to do that right now. All you need to do is decide to be the one who controls your life. No one else, just you. You can do this with affirmations. (There are other methods we will use in conjunction with affirmations and I will mention them shortly and throughout the book).

Affirmations can be said over and over in your head. In fact, every time you have a negative thought you must stop thinking it immediately and replace it with an affirmation. They can be written down. This is good, especially in the beginning, as it imprints the affirmations into your subconscious to write them. They can also be said out loud or even sung. Start, and finish, every day by saying out loud, a positive affirmation about yourself and to yourself in a mirror. It's the most powerful way to start and finish the day ever! Look straight into your eyes in the mirror and say something like "I love me (your name), I love my beauty, my power and my successful life". This is very empowering.

Your eyes are the windows to your soul (your sub-conscious) and there is nothing more powerful than giving your sub-conscious a direct message of self-love to start and finish the day. A mixture of all of the above is probably the best way to go. Begin by writing out your affirmations, say them out loud into the mirror day and night, say them in your head whenever you have a negative thought, sing them in the car or shower or where ever. (If you see a mirror at anytime during the day then you can use it and say your affirmation. You can't say them enough. There is never "too much".)

During this whole process you must be vigilant and disciplined. You must notice EVERY time you have a negative thought and replace it with a positive one. You must also make sure that you begin to be positive and happy even when you're not saying your affirmations. Your affirmations will not work if you say them and, when you've finished, you go back to being depressed or down hearted. You must change your whole way of thinking for things to physically change in your world. Life's equation goes like this:

First there is thought: (which creates);

Ideas: (which creates);

The physical end product.

You can't get a new car and have that create a whole new positive attitude for you. It'll make you excited for a few days until the novelty wears off. Then you'll be back to square one, looking for the next "thing" to cheer you up. No, you must first change the way that you think which will, in turn, create a new world for you which will, in turn, bring new "things" into your life.

One of the greatest indicators of insanity is for someone to repeat the same action, over and over again, and expecting a different outcome to occur. To create a different ***outcome*** in our lives we must first change our ***actions.*** Our ***actions*** occur because of our ***belief system***. Our ***belief system*** is made up of our ***thoughts***. Therefore, changing your ***thoughts*** changes your ***belief system*** which, in turn, changes your ***actions*** which, ultimately, will create different ***outcomes***.

It all begins with your thoughts. The best way to change your thoughts is through the use of affirmations. This is the way it works and affirmations are the most powerful and most successful tool to be used in changing the way you think about yourself and your life. A positive attitude is the only way to bring about positive change in your life. Simple as that. In part two of this book I've given you affirmations for different issues or conditions that may have affected your life. These affirmation are included as part of the healing process as whole. What you can do is take any affirmations that you deem pertinent for you or that resonate with you and use them well. You can keep changing them as you see fit.

Learn to be silent,
Let your mind
Listen and absorb

PYTHAGORUS

MEDITATION

MEDITATION IS AN ESSENTIAL TOOL in achieving a stress-free, happy and enlightened life. It's also very important in terms of achieving a state of total and unconditional self-love. What we're saying to ourselves when we meditate is that we are worthy of the time we take to just "be". To just sit with ourselves and give ourselves the gift of complete and utter rest. Free from the incessant "inner chatter" that goes on day and night whether we like it, or are totally aware of it, or not!

It only needs to be twenty minutes a day. If you can do that twice a day then all the better. But don't stress over it! That would be totally counterproductive. As you progress with your meditative practice you'll find the time to do more than twenty minutes. You'll be able to meditate for forty, fifty minutes and even an hour with it seeming to only go for two minutes or so in duration. When you allow yourself to relax into a deep meditation then time absolutely flies! However, to begin with, twenty minutes once a day will suffice. Just find a quiet space, probably at home, but if there's a space to be used at your work place then great, and give yourself the gift of twenty minutes devoted just to you. No-one else but you.

It has been stated that half an hour of meditation is the equivalent of about four hours of sleep. Even in your deepest sleep your subconscious mind is working. It's where your dreams are coming from. So your mind does not get the complete rest it truly needs. Meditation does that though. When you can still your mind in meditation you will then enjoy complete and utter rest.

There are many styles of meditation. All of them are valid. What you need to do is find the style that best suits you. I have found the best for me is to use the very simple breathing based meditation but with a "twist". I play some of the wonderful meditation music that can be found readily and I use crystals and other tokens either on my person or I hold them while I meditate. What is advisable is for you to find some local meditation classes, preferably guided ones to begin with, and meditate with a group first. Guided meditations are a great way to get yourself into the meditating habit. You will also discover a lot about yourself through this method and will begin the healing process.

The simplest form of meditation is to find a space where you won't be interrupted and just sit. Make sure you're sitting comfortably. A chair or lounge is fine as long as your back is straight and your feet are comfortably placed on the ground. If you can sit crossed legged or even in the lotus position then that's fine too. Or if you've got crystals placed on, lets say, your third eye chakra (the spot in between your eyes) then you're more likely to be lying down, and that's fine also. There are no hard and fast rules as to what is the best position to be in. Being comfortable is paramount. When you're in a perfectly comfortable position, then begin to concentrate on the breath going in and out and try not to think of anything. Don't be hard on yourself if you can't "just think of nothing." You probably won't ever clear your mind entirely of thoughts but it's the striving for that state that's the important action here. So, try to completely clear your head of all of the everyday thoughts you have. As thoughts come into your head then thank them for coming but let them go and go back to attempting to be thinking of nothing. Just focus on the breath flowing in and out and in and out. After a while time will fly and your twenty minutes or so will be over and only seem like two minutes! Don't be disheartened if you don't feel you achieve a peaceful state or if you have trouble keeping the thoughts away. It'll come as long as you persist. It's just practice as with learning any sport or musical instrument.

What we do when we meditate is plug ourselves straight into the greater- consciousness and avail ourselves of all the information and healing powers gathered there in absolute abundance. So whenever we meditate, we heal. That just happens. What we can do as we become more and more proficient at meditating is we can tailor our meditations to suit the different issues we're facing at any given time. In fact I'll give you a specific meditation at the end of each chapter through the book which will relate directly to the issue or topic of that particular chapter.

As you begin your meditation you can ask for healing. You can call on whoever means something to you as in "Angels", "the greater-consciousness", "I AM", "God" etc. Whatever, and whoever, is important and works for you. For me they are all one and the same anyway. Simply put, they are all part and parcel of "the source", that spiritual source of healing and divinity. It exists. We only have to believe it and tap into it. So, before you meditate on any issues or conditions that you want healing for, you simply ask your "source" to come and give you healing on that issue or condition while you're meditating. Then you can go into your meditation and allow the healing to take its natural course. You may feel or sense something happening to you during your meditation or you may experience nothing at all. It doesn't matter. If you have belief and you ask for healing then no matter what your experience is, you will be given healing. It's all about trust. In time enough evidence will show itself to you for you to trust without question. Just do me one favour and never give up. Keep going even when the going gets tough. Remember, "The only way through, is through". You will see and feel the benefits of this work. There is no doubt about that as long as you stick to the task, "put in the hard yards" and keep going no matter what. If you do the work you will reap the benefits. Remember there is no such thing as failure. Every meditation, even if you think it's been totally ineffectual, will be doing you some good.

Another fantastic aid in your healing process is to use crystals. You can discover what crystals may be pertinent to whatever it is you're healing at any given time and you can hold them or place them, comfortably and conveniently, on your person while you meditate. Crystals are very powerful. They have incredible energy properties. This has been scientifically and anecdotally proven over the centuries. So find out about the properties attributed to individual crystals and use them lovingly to aid your healing.

To begin with here are the qualities of some popular crystals:

Clear Quartz: (Colour: Clear) Is an excellent crystal to be used during meditation. It receives, activates, stores, transforms, transmits and amplifies energy and thought into form. It's also used for emotional balance and it dispels negativity and stimulates brain functions.

Amethyst: (Violet) The Amethyst is a great crystal for enhancing right brain activity. It's also used a lot in meditation. It can help to clear and transform energies in the environment where it's placed. It's a very protective crystal. It also enhances psychic abilities and spiritual awareness.

Tiger Eye: (Golden Brown) Tiger eye will aid in grounding, centering and will soften stubbornness. It also enhances personal power.

Hematite: (Grey to Black) Hematite promotes tranquillity and emotional clarity. It can also strengthen physical and etheric bodies. It's also brilliant for mental attunement.

Celestite: (Light Blue) This crystal helps to clear all of your left brain clutter. It helps you connect with your higher being. It also helps to empty the mind, ease doubt and accelerate growth, particularly spiritual.

Green Aventurine:
(Green) Your health and well being will be improved by this crystal. It'll also help you to move on from a limited idea of what you're capable of. It's also really helpful in career assessment and changes in your life. It can enhance your positive attitude and your emotional tranquillity. This is a really good "all-round" healing crystal.

Aquamarine: (Light-Blue to Blue) Aquamarine teaches you to see yourself as worthy. It' a very reassuring and uplifting crystal It promotes the clarity of your mind and is very good for balance on all levels. It's great for dealing with and overcoming fears and phobias. It also can give off feelings of inspiration, peace and love.

The most obvious and beneficial areas on the body to place your crystals are on your Chakra points. For the uninitiated I'll give a brief description of them right here:

We all have seven major Chakra, or energy, points situated throughout our bodies. The lowest one is the "**Base**" or "**Root**" Chakra which is situated on the perineum (the space between the anus and the genitals). This point relates to issues of survival, the material plane, status in life, balance and so on. All Chakra's have a colour and in the case of the base Chakra the colour, when the Chakra is operating perfectly and healthily, is red. (All of the Chakra's take on a "dirtier" or cloudy type of hue when they're not operating at 100%).

The next one is the **Sacral** Chakra. This is positioned just above the pubic hairline on top of the genitals. This point is concerned with issues of sexuality, emotions, guilt, blame and creativity. This Chakra's colour is orange.

The next is the **Solar Plexus**. This is the navel area. (Your belly button). The issues here are inner power, will and confidence, fear and decision-making. The colour here is yellow.

The **Heart** Chakra is next and this is positioned in the middle of your chest in your heart area. The issues are love, relationships, compassion and grief. The colour is green.

Next is the **Throat** Chakra. This is obviously on your throat area. The main issues here are self-expression, speaking your truth and communication. The colour is blue.

The **Third Eye**, or **Brow**, Chakra is next. The issues here are imagination, intuition, clarity of thought, and dreams. The colour is indigo.

The last Chakra point is the **Crown** Chakra. This one is situated right on top of your head and relates to issues of understanding, higher consciousness, universal identity and the colour is Violet.

So, they go like this:

CROWN	(TOP OF THE HEAD)
THIRD EYE	(BROW)
THROAT	(THROAT)
HEART	(CENTRE CHEST, LEVEL WITH HEART)

SOLAR PLEXUS	(BELLY BUTTON)
SACRAL	(PUBIC BONE)
BASE	(BETWEEN GENITALS AND ANUS)

As you can see, finding out about the properties associated with particular crystals and then applying them and placing them on the pertinent Chakra points can be an amazingly successful tool in healing. Especially when used in conjunction with meditation. So, pinpoint the issue/condition/problem you may have, find the perfect crystal that relates, place that crystal on the related Chakra point and then call on your "source" for healing, put on your beautiful meditation music and meditate away into healing heaven. Constant practice of these healing skills and information will transform and change your life forever.

Probably the most important point to consider here is that by just contemplating giving yourself the time and energy to take on these healing principles means you are saying, very loudly and very clearly, that you are WORTHY of the time and energy it takes to heal yourself. So, well done! You're already on the path to self-love. Now, keep going!

All we see or seem,
Is but a dream within a dream

EDGAR ALLEN POE

VISUALIZATION

VISUALIZATION IS ANOTHER equally important tool to be used in the redirection of your life. If you want to take your life in a new positive direction then you will need to visualize. What is visualization? Basically it's a bit like meditation. It's all about finding the time for yourself which, as I've already said, is very important in itself, and seeing your new golden future as if you are living it right now.

If you want to be more financially secure in your life then you need to take a little time each and every day and see yourself already having that financial security. Whatever form that takes for you, that's what you need to see. This is the only way you'll have that new security. It won't come otherwise. If you want more money but keep seeing yourself as poor then the new money won't come to you. It won't enter a poverty consciousness environment. If you want a new home then sit and visualize yourself already in that new home and it will come to you. If you want a new job or promotion then visualize that new job and promotion and, along with all the other work you'll do here, that job and promotion will be yours. It's all about aiding our positive thinking. We are what we think. If we can see ourselves as already achieving our goals then our sub-conscious will believe it to be true. Our sub-conscious cannot tell the difference between visualizing something or actually having it. Therefore our thoughts will be informed to the affirmative. Our thoughts will dictate our actions. This is how we attract the "new" into our lives. Again I'll set visualizations which will directly relate to each issue from each chapter.

Each player must accept,
The card's life deals him or her:
But once they are in hand,
He or she alone must decide,
How to play the cards,
In order to win the game.

VOLTAIRE

RESPONSIBILTY

WE MUST TAKE RESPONSIBILITY for all of our actions and words in our lives. This is the only way we will be set free. Taking total responsibility for ones words and actions is the most liberating thing one can do.

As I've already mentioned, taking responsibility is essential in terms of achieving a state of complete unconditional self-love, and visa-versa. When you achieve a state of self-love you can't help but take complete responsibility for all of your words and actions and you allow everyone else to do the same. It's totally and unequivocally liberating. It frees you completely. No-one can have any form of control over you when you take responsibility for all your actions and your words. You've nothing to hide then.

Taking responsibility stops you from blaming others for whatever happens to be going on with you. In fact, blame can become a very good barometer as to how well you're taking responsibility. If you find yourself putting blame out there you can stop and notice why you're doing it: knowing it's really you that has the "problem" not the people you're blaming. You can then deal with that "problem" using whatever healing technique it requires and move further on to a state of complete self-love.

A brilliant tool in terms of taking responsibility for one's life is summed up by the following two quotes: "Everything happens for a reason" and "There are no coincidences". These are both amazing statements with huge ramifications. When we realize and truly believe that everything does happen for a reason and that there really are no coincidences then we're totally in a position to accept full responsibility for our own lives.

This state frees us from being a victim. We're no longer at the mercy of the fates. We can't say anymore, "oh that's just bad luck" or "why won't things go right for me?" or "It's not my fault, these things just happen". We can't say that because in some way, shape or form we are responsible for everything that happens to us in our lives. We have brought about every occurrence in our lives by our thoughts. Obviously negative thoughts will tend to bring on negative occurrences and positive thoughts will bring on positive occurrences. Another famous quote sums up this situation: "As you think, so shall you be".

We've got to look at what's happening in our lives at any given point and work out what we're doing, thinking and saying, to bring it all about. We've also got to look at how we handle all the situations that arise in our lives. It's not what happens to us in this life but, rather, how we react to what happens to us that is the measure of us. In other words, if something negative occurs in our lives and we crumble and fail to cope then that shows that we're living with a victim mentality. If, however, something negative occurs in our lives and we simply take it in our stride, look at it closely, identify what we've done to create the situation, learn from it and move on, then that shows that we're living in a state of self-love and taking full responsibility for our lives. That's a wonderful state to be in. You will be free and very powerful in that state.

Knowing that everything happens for a reason, and that there are no coincidences, allows you to look for sign-posts in your life. When something occurs in your life and then something similar occurs soon after and then something similar soon after that, and so on, then that's the universe sending you a message. You must look out for these signs and decipher the messages in order to obtain greater insight into your purpose in this life. For instance, let's say you're contemplating joining a gym. You're mulling it over but you're not quite sure. Then, one day a friend, who has never been a fitness freak, calls you up and tells you they've won a gym membership and would you like to go along once and be a guest with them. Then, on another occasion soon after, you notice a new gym has just opened up very near to you with advertising signs offering discounts for early joiners. Soon after that you're watching television and you stumble on a documentary which details the wonderful benefits of weight bearing exercise.

These three occurrences are not accidents or coincidences. They have all happened for a reason and that reason is for you to follow your initial gut reaction and join the gym. Now the long term reason for this could be, not just to get fit, trim and terrific, although they are very good reasons on their own. But it may be that you will meet your true love at that gym, or you may discover and fall in love with, let's say, aerobics, and it becomes a crucial and very important part of your life, or you may meet someone in the locker room, and find out that your business interests are the same and you embark on a profitable new venture with them. The possibilities are endless. The point is, watch for the signs, know that everything happens for a reason and use the information you're being given wisely.

The shortest way
To do many things
Is to do
Only one thing
At once

SAMUAL SMILES

BREATHING

ARE YOU BREATHING RIGHT NOW? Well of course you are or you'd be dead, right? Of course, that's over-stating the obvious isn't it? But what is not always obvious is *how* you are breathing. Too many people take breathing for granted and are not aware of how or where they breathe.

There are many different ways to breathe. We can all become short of breath, breathe deeply, huff and puff during exercise and so on. But how often are we aware of why we're breathing the way we are for a particular reason in a given situation? I would suggest not often enough.

Breathing is crucial to our state of mind and our physical well-being as well. It's everything really. It's probably the most important function of our lives and one we take for granted far too often. We need to know *how*, *why* and *where* we breathe. For instance, if we're breathing into our chests alone then that's called shallow breathing. That will maintain a state of anxiety within us. We're not in a state of great control with that way of breathing. Too many people breathe this way all the time though. Even when they think they're relaxed they still breathe in a shallow way. What are needed are big deep breaths that fill out the lungs and centre the body.

Stand up right now. Put your hand on your tummy, right over the top of your belly button. Now breathe in deeply and push your hand out. Don't let your chest lift or push out and don't let your shoulders lift. Nothing should move but your hand, in and out with the fall and rise of your stomach. Can you do it? If you can then that's good. You're breathing correctly. If you can't then you've got some work to do.

Practice this way of breathing all the time. Be aware of how you're breathing and notice when it changes from a deep, relaxed breathing to shallow breathing and then bring it back to the deep. This form of deep breathing is where all your power is. It's your centre, your chi. It's balancing and calming to breathe in this way. Any other way is incorrect and detrimental to your general well-being. So be vigilant and watch how you breathe.

Meditating will help immensely with your breathing. You can't meditate without breathing deeply into your tummy and filling up your lungs. But what we don't want is the situation where you breathe deeply when meditating and then just go back to bad breathing practices in your every day existence. Not good. We don't want that. You really must focus on it and make sure you're grounded all the time by making sure you get that breath going down, deep into your gut. Make sure you're coming from your power position at all times. It's essential. So happy, deep breathing folks.

How does it get any better than this!

BOBBY RUNNING FOX

GRATITUDE

TO ALLOW THE "NEW" AND ABUNDANCE into our lives we must first establish a state of gratefulness in the here and now......the present. This is all we have right now. Yesterday is gone. There is nothing we can do about it. It is in the past.

Tomorrow hasn't arrived yet. We can make plans, set goals and look forward to tomorrow, but that's about it.

Now is all we have and we have to be happy in the now. It's a gift. That's why it's called the "present". So we need to be grateful for the gift of the present and be happy in the moment. I know this is easy to say and a lot harder to do but it's something that must be striven for and achieved for personal growth and happiness.

Before going to sleep and immediately upon awakening, are two prime times to thank the universe for everything you have in your life right now. I bet if you stop and take stock you'll find that your life is rich and abundant. Abundance comes in many more ways than just monetarily. I'll bet you have family who love you. A mother, a father, brothers, sisters, aunts, uncles and cousins. You may have a significant other who loves you very much. Possibly even children. (There's nothing quite like the unconditional love of the young). A dog, a cat or some other lovable pet. Friends. We all have friends that love us whether we're in touch with them all the time or not. Friends may as well be put in the family bracket as far as I'm concerned. We're all family really. Wherever you look I bet you can find an abundance of love and good will around you. If you say no to that right now then I reckon you're not looking quite hard enough. Keep looking, you'll find it.

If you have a roof over your head, clothes to wear, money in your pocket, food to eat, water to drink, books to read, then you are immensely abundant. A large part of the world's population only has very little, if any of the above mentioned luxuries. In fact just being on top of the ground and breathing is a reason to feel grateful! So, know this every day and be thankful. This state of gratefulness is an essential and wonderful platform to launch your happiness from. Be grateful and be happy...in the moment. In the present. Right now! Not tomorrow, or the next day. Not when you have that new car you want, the new job, new haircut, more money, different house, etc. NO! BE HAPPY NOW! The only person holding you back is you.

One of the most positive affirmations which immediately puts us in a state of gratefulness, even when we're feeling really down and out is this;

"How does it get any better than this?"

Use this affirmation all the time. When things don't seem

to be going right. When you feel like life is unfair. When you're having the typical "bad day". Use this affirmation. Say, "How does it get any better than this" and watch it all turn around. You simply can't feel down when you're in a state of gratefulness and this one simple phrase puts you into that state. It's a beauty. Use it well.

All the world's a stage,
And all the men and women merely players,
They have their exits and their entrances,
And one man in his time plays many parts

WILLIAM SHAKESPEARE

PAST LIVES

THIS TOPIC IS GOING TO BE A BIT OF A "LEAP" for some people. For others it won't be so hard and for some, it's just the norm. I don't know where you fit on that scale but all I ask is, if you're unsure of past life stuff, then don't be afraid. Don't be put off either. I simply ask you to give this section a read and make up your own mind at the end. And there's no pressure to believe in past lives either. I do, and it creates an understanding for me for this life and beyond. Other people believe in heaven and hell. I don't. But I don't judge them and, I hope, they don't judge me. We're all on this planet, at this time, together, so let's just get on and get *on* with it. Ok, so read on with an open mind and an open heart.

Past lives are important, as they are all part of the journey of our soul. This is the journey to enlightenment. True enlightenment, in my opinion, is when we've discovered and accepted total and unconditional self-love. When we've torn away all of the layers of negativity. When we achieve enlightenment then we're ready to become part of the light, the source, the knowledge, whatever you want to call it in accordance with your belief system, in any case it's the place where all enlightened souls exist in light. Completely and utterly free. Where no time exists. Where the norm is being in all places at once. There is nothing but love, happiness, bliss.

Funnily enough this state can take many lives to achieve. I believe that if we don't deal with certain negative states of mind and body in one life then we'll be given the same issues and tests in the next life, and then the next, until we finally acknowledge the "sign-posts" and deal with whatever it is we have to deal with.

In each and every one of our lives we're striving to discover the true path to enlightenment, to true self-love. Therefore, if it hasn't happened in one life then the journey, from the point it is up to, will continue in the next. That's the baggage we carry. So we not only carry the hurts and negative input that occurs in this life, we carry with us the hurts and negative inputs that we haven't yet dealt with from our previous lives as well.

This all affects our self-esteem. Our ability to love ourselves unconditionally. It's obvious that the path to complete unconditional self-love is a steep and cluttered one and that patience and hard work are needed. Again, healing is needed. Past life issues can be healed in the same way as present life issues. (see chapter on healing) It's all just another facet of the work we need to do on ourselves to completely, and without ego, truly love ourselves. We all deserve the great gift of self-love so let's do all the work we can, in this life, to achieve it.

Part Two

Your Issues
And How To Heal Them

INDEX

To find yourself,
Think for yourself

SOCRATES

CONDITIONING

ALL OF OUR LIVES WE ARE BOMBARDED with negative information about ourselves. Information that reaffirms, everyday, that we're not really worthy individuals. The media plays a major part in this indoctrination but our families and friends also do their bit. (Albeit unsuspecting in most cases. They're simply victims of the same socialization and don't know any different). Then there are the people who know exactly what they're doing, but that's another story about Karma and strength of character, which is a strong sense of self-love.

Before we are born we take on positive but also negative input from our birth mother as we sit comfortably in the womb. A very close friend of mine has an irrational fear of dogs. He has had it all his life and has never been attacked by a dog. Not once! However, his mother was. When she was carrying him in her womb. Obviously that attack on his mother, the fear she felt as a pregnant woman, fed straight into my friend in the womb and has stuck with him ever since. So too, other negative input will feed into the unborn and stay with them until they learn of its existence and learn how to heal it.

When we are born we are bombarded with negative information about ourselves from birth. In a lot of hospital births, certainly in the recent past, the infant is taken away from the mother and placed in a florescent cubicle with other distressed infants. These first few hours of earth experience, coming from the utterly nurturing environment of the womb, are devastating to an entirely receptive newborn. (We also carry with us whatever negative self-esteem issues are hung-over from past lives). As we grow the significant people in our lives, whilst following the rules of their own negatively corrupted socialization, begin to impart onto us the same negatively corrupt socialization.

Someone will say something to us. Something, (perhaps on the surface), innocuous enough but something that hurts us. On the surface, in our conscious mind, we say " This is OK. It did hurt but I'm tough enough and life goes on", and we do go on. But those hurts, however large or small, slip through to our deep subconscious where they sit and fester until we either become aware of them and heal them out or we let them stay and shape our lives.

So, as you can see, life, through conditioning due to a negatively corrupt socialization, presents us with a constant bombardment of negative input. A bombardment that we have to battle against, and win against with our own inner dialogue of positive input.

If we don't win this battle then this is how we learn to take on stress. Stress which, if allowed to fester and grow, can turn into all kinds of afflictions both mental and physical, and even life threatening dis-ease. (You know the ones. I'm not going to give them credence by mentioning them here).

The first thing we need to do is acknowledge our negative conditioning. I want you to take the time, (the best spent time of your life), and go back over your life from before you were born till now. If your mother is still living then study her or ask her questions about her pregnancy with you. Even if she's passed on you can remember what she was like as a person and so therefore will have a pretty good idea of how she would have handled the stress and rigors of pregnancy and childbirth. This will inform you in terms of what negative input went into the womb during your stay there.

Then I want you to try to remember every hurtful thing that has been said to you in your life up until today. Take your time, this is very important. Some things will be repetitive like a father or a mother or a brother or a sister or other relatives or a teacher, priest, sports coach, constantly telling you you're stupid, ugly, too skinny, too fat, or not good at something, that you're "hopeless", accident prone and so on. The list goes on and on, unfortunately. These repetitive negative comments are the "big" ones obviously but all the other negative things said to you up until now all affect you and create and feed a lack of self-esteem/self-love.

Write down all these negative statements. Don't leave anything out no matter how insignificant you may think it was at the time. It all goes in and it all affects your sub-conscious. What you need to know and have to accept right now is that everything that was said to you in a negative sense throughout all of your life so far has all been lies! Untruths! There is not one skerrick of truth attached to any of them. They are all other peoples perceptions which have been affected by their negative conditioning and have nothing to do with your ability to do anything you want to do in this life.

Now take that piece of paper and rip it into tiny little pieces. Spit on it, stamp on it, do whatever you need to do to treat those negative statements with the contempt they deserve. When you have done that throw the remains of the page into the bin, burn them or dispose of them any way you want. Just get rid of them. They don't exist for you in this life any longer.

Michael Domeyko Rowlands, a world renowned leader in life management, has studied the brain in a clinical sense, has run meditation centres around the world and has changed the lives of many with his "Life Essentials"course and his book "Absolute Happiness". He has a wonderful analogy for these hurts that are within us and how they affect us. I will borrow it here. You know how hard it is to keep a beach ball under the water? Unless you keep an even pressure across the top of the ball it will burst back up through the surface. This is not an easy job. It takes strength, concentration and balance. Well all those hurts are just like beach balls. As each one goes in, it needs to be kept under the surface. In comes the next one, again it's got to be kept under, now another one and another and so on and so on. Until you have a whole lot of beach balls you're trying to keep under the surface inside of you. This is a huge effort. A huge waste of your precious energy. It affects your physical and mental states. It will cause permanent and long term damage unless those beach balls are healed out of you.

So let's look at some healing techniques that apply to issues or problems that arise from conditioning.

AFFIRMATIONS

Some examples of affirmations in regards to negative thoughts due to conditioning are:

- ❑ I love me (your name) I love my (if negative input was "ugly" then put in here, "**Beauty**") my (replace say, "stupid" with "**intelligenc**e") and my (if "hopeless" then replace with "**successful life**").
- ❑ Today is another happy, glorious and successful day in the life of me (your name).
- ❑ I am worthy.
- ❑ I am the most important person in my life.
- ❑ When I change my thoughts I change my world
- ❑ I deserve nothing but the very best.
- ❑ Life supports me when I support myself.
- ❑ My potential is endless.
- ❑ Today is the first day of the rest of my life.
- ❑ I can do whatever it is I want to do
- ❑ I am bold, brave and beautiful
- ❑ I am powerful, prosperous and successful
- ❑ Abundance is mine
- ❑ I am loved and accepted exactly as I am
- ❑ I am never defeated by anyone or anything
- ❑ I seek approval from no one but myself
- ❑ I am beautiful, inside and out

- ❑ There is no failure, only lessons
- ❑ I am happy, right here, right now
- ❑ Feel the fear, and do it anyway
- ❑ The only way through, is through
- ❑ My need to please starts with me

MEDITATION

While using the affirmations in regards to conditioning, a perfect way to meditate would be to sit for 20 minutes a day with some beautifully uplifting music playing and just being completely and utterly still. Just concentrate on your breathing. Notice how you're breath goes in and out, in and out. Keep thanking any thoughts that are coming into your head for being there and continually send them away.

You can ask now for whom ever it is you connect with in terms of a "source" to come and give you healing in terms of issues or problems you may have due to negative conditioning. Know that even if you ask for nothing, just being still and not thinking of anything will connect you to the Greater-Consciousness and will be healing you regardless. Asking for more help just concentrates that healing.

A couple of crystals that would be ideal to be used during this meditation or, indeed, to carry around in regards to issues derived from conditioning are:

Angelite: (colour: light-blue) Angelite can soothe fear and anxiety It also helps with trauma and can give off a feeling of well-being and satisfaction.

Rose Quartz: (pink) Will help to clear stored anger, resentment, guilt, fear and jealousy. It's also a fantastic crystal for enhancing love. In fact it's often referred to as "the love stone". So it works beautifully for self-love.

Angelite is best placed on the throat and/or heart Chakra's in this case and Rose Quartz is best placed on the heart Chakra.

Search out and find more crystals that pertain more individually to you. Visit a crystal shop and see which crystals "jump out" at you. What you will find is that you will be drawn to certain crystals. They are the ones you need for whatever reason at that particular time. Find out what their qualities are and use them accordingly.

When you don't need a certain crystal for a certain issue, in other words, when you have resolved that issue, then that crystal will leave you. It will let you know it no longer needs to be on your person or near you from that point. For example, if you have the crystal on a necklace or a bracelet then, when its job is done, it will most likely break so you can't wear it any more or fall off and basically disappear. So notice this as it's a great indicator that you've moved on in your life and healed whatever it was you were having difficulties with in your life at that time in your life.

VISUALIZATION

Visualization is an important tool in terms of healing with issues and conditions that have arisen due to negative conditioning. So, take some moments throughout your day or night. You only need five minutes at a time really. When you have that five-minutes, find a quiet spot, still yourself and begin to visualize.

For example, if you have an illogical fear of dogs just like my friend then you need to see yourself being totally confident with a group of dogs. See yourself patting them with them returning your affection tenfold.

If you have been conditioned to see yourself as fat, then visualize yourself with a fit and athletic body. Don't see yourself growing into that body, see yourself having it right now. If you've been told you're too thin, then see yourself with that same fit and athletic body right now.

You can do as many visualizations as you want to. In fact, you can't do too many. The more the merrier. The ideal would be for the visualization to seemingly slip into reality without you being completely aware of the transition. The main thing is to never give up. Be diligent and persistent and you will always have positive results.

Man cannot discover new oceans,
Until he has courage,
To lose sight
Of the shore

UNKNOWN

FEAR

FEAR IS ANOTHER INDICATOR of a lack of self-love. Fear can block us from enjoying various life experiences that could enhance our self-esteem. In other words, by not taking part in some activities because we're "scared" is another way of saying, "I'm not worthy enough to take part". Saying "I'm too scared" is another way of saying "I'm not good enough". Obviously there are some natural, instinctive fears that we need to retain such as a healthy fear of sharks, bad guys in balaclava's wielding knives and war zones. I'm talking about fears such as not taking that promotion because you're frightened you couldn't handle the responsibility. Not going out because you're too scared to walk into a night-club/pub/party alone. Not going on that holiday for fear of something going wrong while you're away. Not being able to stand up in front of people in a public speaking setting. Not being able to sing in front of people. Obviously there are many more instances where fear blocks our growth because we don't think we are worthy. We've got one or a few fears tucked away inside of us. Sometimes we're not even aware of them. We just know we don't like something for whatever reason. We've never been drawn to jump out of airplanes or bungy jump or even cook a dinner party for friends. They're just things we don't do. We don't realize that deep down we're too frightened to do those things. Sometimes we block ourselves from an exciting and fulfilling life experience, due to our fears.

You need to pinpoint your fears. You need to be very honest and brave and face up to some of these fears. It's easier to be called "tough" and say, "I'm OK Jack! I'm not frightened of anything really". Well we all know that's not real! We've all got fears. "The only way through, is through" but you can't get "through" anything if you haven't identified it first. So come on, let's be really brave and honestly point out our fears. Sometimes perceived as weaknesses but that's not true. They're just fears. Nothing else. Let's learn how to deal with them, face them, heal and eradicate them.

We tend to carry our fear in our gut. In our belly. That's what those old "butterflies" are. That's how sometimes we can become so scared we can actually be physically ill. Fear is a build up of all the negative inner-chatter that's been going on and on for, sometimes, years. This negative speak filters down and tends to lodge in the stomach where we store it. Obviously some very deep seated and amplified fears can actually, in certain instances, totally freeze our entire bodies and not allow us to move or take any action at that time. We need to heal this. We can't live our lives in fear. We can't go through life always playing it safe. That is akin to locking ourselves in our own protective prisons. They may feel safe and comforting and protective but they will be prisons nonetheless.

That's no way to live. By playing it safe we'll simply re-run our old debilitating patterns. We won't get anywhere. We must unlock our prisons and get out there and experience this life to the fullest. We owe it to ourselves. We must "Feel the Fear, and Do It Anyway"! (Also the title of a fantastic book by Susan Jeffers which I highly recommend). Facing our fears and breaking through them enhances our self-esteem, which, in turn, enhances our resolve to face and conquer more fears which will, inevitably enable us to be free from fear and able to lead the wonderful lives we all know we're supposed to be living! Once you conquer one fear there is exponential growth and fear after fear will begin to fall in all the areas of your life.

So to heal your fears you need to, firstly (and honestly), identify them. Don't be silly and "brave" and deny your fears. That's simply very unhelpful. It won't get you anywhere. Identify your fears. That's a liberating act in itself. Once you've done that you need to begin the healing process.

AFFIRMATIONS

Some affirmations that deal wonderfully with fear issues are:

- Feel the fear and do it anyway
- The only way through is through
- I am not afraid of anyone or anything
- I release all my fears and doubts
- I see every difficulty as a challenge
- I will never be defeated by anyone or anything
- I am safe, secure and successful
- I'm not better than anybody else, and nobody is better then me
- I am brave, strong and resilient
- I am a warrior
- There is nothing to fear, but fear itself
- 99% of everything I worry about never happens
- I can handle anything
- I am safe, I am happy and I love my life

MEDITATION

1. Identify the fears that you want to heal.
2. Find your quiet space and time.
3. Put on your meditation music, ask for healing from your "source" in terms of your fear issues.
4. Relax, focus on your breath and allow yourself to drift away to a place of total relaxation, release and healing.

A few crystals that would be ideal to use during this meditation or to carry around in regards to issues derived from fear are:

Tourmaline: (Tourmaline comes in many colours. The best one to use in terms of fear is the Rubellite Tourmaline which is usually pink and red) This is a powerful healing stone. It fights fear and all negative influences. It also has very strong protective qualities.

Sodalite: (A bright blue stone, often crisscrossed with white and grey lines) Sodalite alleviates fear. It can also calm and clear the mind.

Malachite: (A layered green, opaque stone) This stone helps you to discover the root of your fears. It then helps to eradicate them.

Aquamarine (Light blue to blue) Aquamarine works best by helping to banish fears and phobias. It also promotes feelings of inspiration, calmness, peace and love.

The Rubellite Tourmaline is best placed on the Heart Chakra. The Sodalite is best on the Throat or Third eye Chakra. The Malachite is best on the Solar Plexus/Heart Chakras and the Aquamarine is best on the Throat Chakra.

VISUALIZATION

In terms of combating, overcoming and healing your fears, visualization will be a crucial tool. As already mentioned, take your five minute breaks anytime during the day or night and sit, be still, close your eyes and see yourself doing or saying the very things you're currently frightened to do or say. Your mind can't decide between visualizing something and actually having that something. So if you believe it and visualize it often enough you will get it, whatever it is you want.

In this case, after visualizing for a while, you'll suddenly find yourself actually doing and saying the things you were previously frightened of. However, you're obviously not going to do or say anything that is going to have a negative impact on another. Whether that be a spouse, boss, friend, family member or work-mate. That's not going to work at all. That defeats the purpose entirely. You're here to heal yourself and move on to be a better and more fulfilled person, you're not here to be the cause of another persons fears, negative thoughts or low self-esteem. So only ever come from your heart. Speak and act out your truth without judgment, blame, ego and revenge being involved. Take responsibility for your actions and words and allow all others to do the same. Let's get the passion out of the equation and replace it with respect. That's always going to make it a 'win, win" situation for all involved.

Life is either,
A daring adventure,
Or nothing

HELEN KELLER

SEXUAL FREEDOM

INTIMACY AND SEXUAL FREEDOM of expression and sexual enjoyment also suffer due to a lack of self-love. Intimacy, for example, is all about commitment. And commitment is all about being able to feel worthy enough to know that we deserve to love and be loved. Historically men have a problem with intimacy. This goes back to the issue of socialization. Boys are brought up to be tough and independent. But what that does, deep down in the sub-conscious of the boy, is tell him he's got to be tough because he doesn't deserve to need anyone or have anyone need him. This is obviously wrong. We all deserve to give and receive commitment (intimacy/love).

Girls, conversely, are taught that it's OK for the man to be in a relationship with her without having to commit. He will sleep with her, father her children, work hard and provide a home all without intimacy. Her job is to give him whatever he needs, physically and emotionally, so that he can provide all that he's supposed to. She also has to provide, physically and emotionally, everything her children need to become good citizens. All the while her needs, her acknowledgment as a worthy person through intimacy (commitment), are neglected. Not only are they neglected but also she is taught that she has no right to that acknowledgment.

Censorship laws back this up 100 percent. The way film and TV is rated completely sends out the wrong message. Violence always achieves a lower rating than programs containing explicit sex scenes. So the connotation is that sex is dirty and bad but violence is OK! This is the message that winds its way into our collective psyche and buries itself there. (As a point of interest Sweden has virtually no censorship on the sexual content of its film and TV and has virtually no rape either.)

So our culture teaches us that we're not worthy of intimacy but we're worthy of inflicting pain upon others. This is totally all around the wrong way. Censorship bodies are largely made up of middle aged men who are products of corrupt socialization who really don't know any better but to repeat the mistakes of the past. It won't be until there is a lot of healing throughout society that changes will be able to be made in this and many other areas.

Sex is not dirty! On the contrary, it is one of the most beautiful acts of sharing we have. Ideally a fulfilling and totally satisfying sexual experience will be all about two people sharing in terms of telling each other what each others needs are. Too many people don't think that they're worthy of speaking up and saying that if you do "that" to me then I'm going to have a fantastic orgasm. Or, what is it that I can do to give you a fantastic orgasm? The sexual experience should be a joyous and exciting one. It shouldn't be about doing what one thinks is right because it's what we've been taught from our parents. "Just give him what he needs and he won't stray" This is just not good enough. This is a huge lack of self-love working overtime.

Find your own beauty within and you will see so very clearly the beauty in others. Find your self-love and you will love to love others and you will never allow yourself to settle for second-best, especially when it comes to sexual freedom, enjoyment and expression.

Also remember that safe sex is a must. If you're enjoying casual sex then the old saying is a true saying, "If it's not on, it's not on"! Condoms are your friend. They're also another measure of your self worth. You are worthy of enjoying casual sex and being completely safe. No one can take that self-love away from you. No one, most certainly, is worth that risk. You're better than that. Don't stand for anyone attempting to get you to take the risk of practicing unsafe sex purely for his or her own selfish reasons. That's just "not on"!

AFFIRMATIONS

- ❑ (This one should be done in the mirror morning and night. Stand there, naked, in front of the mirror and say) I love my body, I love my beauty and I love my sexuality.
- ❑ I am open to new sexual experience
- ❑ Sex is fun
- ❑ I deserve to love and to be loved
- ❑ I am surrounded by love and affection
- ❑ I am beautiful and I am loved
- ❑ I have a wonderful lover
- ❑ I am a wonderful lover
- ❑ I love sex
- ❑ I am free to explore my sexuality
- ❑ I enjoy my sexual freedom
- ❑ Enjoying sex is my right
- ❑ I love and adore my body
- ❑ Sex is sharing
- ❑ Sexual joy is my right
- ❑ Sexual freedom is my right
- ❑ Sexual satisfaction is my right

MEDITATION

1 Identify your sexual issues that you want to heal.
2. Find your quiet space and time.
3. Put on your meditation music and ask for healing from your "source" in terms of your sexual issues.
4. Relax, focus on your breath and allow yourself to drift away to a place of total relaxation, release and healing.

A few crystals that would be ideal to be used during this meditation or, indeed, to carry around in regards to issues derived from sexual freedom are:

Smoky Quartz: (It ranges from deep black to brown to yellowy brown) The smoky quartz crystal can start the movement of the primal forces in the body. It also increases fertility and balances sexual energy.

Prase: (Green. Often found with brown markings from matrix rock) Prase is very useful for resolving issues of sexuality and easing sexual guilt. It's also beneficial to the reproductive and sexual organs.

Lepidolite: (Appears in the form of masses, mica-like layers and tabular crystals) Lepidolite helps to open the heart and to promote self-love and the love of others. It's also very calming and soothing.

Rose Quartz: (pink) Helps clear stored anger, resentment, guilt, fear and jealousy. It also promotes love. It's often referred to as "the love stone". So it works beautifully for self-love.

Prase, lepidolite and rose quartz crystals are all best placed on the heart chakra for Maximum results. Smoky Quartz is best place on the base or root chakra.

VISUALIZATION

Again, visualization is an important tool in healing and for change. As always, grab your five minute breaks in the day or night, find a quiet spot where you won't be disturbed, quieten your mind, be still and start to visualize. In terms of sexual freedom, expression and enjoyment issues you should see yourself achieving sexual satisfaction in whatever area of your sex life you currently have an issue, problem or block.

If you haven't been able to achieve orgasm then you need to see yourself having the best orgasm you could possibly imagine. See very clearly everything your partner does to help bring you to that climax. See and feel very clearly what changes you make in your own mind which affects your body so that you can finally respond to stimulation that was, perhaps, previously unsuccessful.

Even if you find it hard to initiate sexual contact with your partner, then see yourself, clearly, confidently and successfully doing just that. The list goes on. The most important thing to concentrate on when dealing with your sex life is to focus on enjoyment without guilt. If that is an issue for you then visualize yourself enjoying sex in exactly the way you're not supposed to and then see yourself afterwards being totally satiated and happy and having no guilt whatsoever. Sex is not dirty! It's beautiful. See it that way.

Faith is an oasis,
In the heart,
Which will never be reached,
By the caravan of thinking

KAHLIL GIBRAN

POPULAR CULTURE AND SELF ESTEEM

EVERYWHERE WE TURN THE WORLD is impacting negatively on our self-esteem. Fashion, TV, radio, popular film, popular music, everywhere. Images are thrust upon us in a never ending stream teaching us how we should look, what we should wear, how we should speak, how we should behave, what we should eat, drink, and so on. It's endless and the real problem is we don't know it's all feeding deep into our sub-conscious and controlling our thought patterns. So, ultimately, if we don't wear the right clothes, have the right hairstyle or drive the right car then we're not worthy human beings.

Magazine covers are forever telling women that their bodies and faces must always resemble a 14 year old nymph. Skinny super-models do nothing but promote eating disorders. Muscle bound men on movies, on the television and in pop groups etc, cause millions of young men around the world to over indulge in steroid usage. Now don't get me wrong, I'm not blaming anyone involved in the negative stereotypes I've just identified. They're doing whatever it is they have to do to get through in their lives. That's their journey and good luck to them. What we have to find is enough self-love so that we are not taken in and manipulated by those negative stereotypes.

If we want to have a fit and athletic body it's because we love ourselves enough to know that a good diet and adequate exercise is going to keep us alive longer and help us to enjoy this life while we're still here. So our fit and athletic body has come about due to love, not ego. If we love ourselves enough then we'll wear clothes that we think look really good on us. Not what the popular culture says we should be wearing. The world of fashion is consumerism gone mad. The designers can't make more money if they haven't got you brain washed that life won't be worth living if you don't have this year's designs on your back. That's just ridiculous. If you have good quality clothing and, in your opinion, it looks really good on you, then why wouldn't you wear it until it begins to wear out?

I have certain pieces of clothing where I do just that. With the rest, I monitor it and if I'm not wearing something very often at all anymore then I give it to the charities for someone else to make good use of it. This works on a number of spiritual fronts. Yes it's good karma to give but also making room in your wardrobe allows space for the "new" to come into your life in other areas also. At the same time you are actively involving yourself in your "community" in a wonderfully positive and sharing sense as your clothes are going to be very welcome to someone who is perhaps less fortunate than yourself.

The weight of popular culture expectation can become a burden too hard to bear for some. In fact the stress of trying to be a worthy person according to popular culture can end in tragic circumstances. The unacceptably high rate of teenage suicide is an indicator of just how stressful it can be.

The answer is to look within for worthiness. Again, this is an easy thing to say and a much harder thing to do. It takes work. Lots of work. But who's not prepared to work hard for the greatest cause of all? One's own happiness. How many people think that that's not such a great cause? Don't worry if you don't. You won't be alone. I wrote it just now and didn't believe it myself for a second. But it's just another huge indicator of how we are constantly taught to put ourselves second, third, fourth and so on. Well no! That's just not good enough. We deserve much better than that. We deserve and we are worthy of being put first!

Being first is the only place for us. Without ego. There must never be any ego involved. So that it doesn't become "I'm No.1 and the rest of you can go jump!" It has to become "I'm No.1 and so are the rest of you." To ourselves, we're all No.1's. We're all responsible for our own happiness and in that way we create more happiness wherever we go.

Being No.1 is our right. It's not something we have to wait for someone to give us. We don't have to win a race or some other kind of competition to get to be No.1. We are, and have been No.1 forever. We have just let it slip in our conscious every day thoughts. The constant barrage of negativity pushes us back down the leader board until we hardly count at all to ourselves. We must learn that we are doing no-one any favours by letting ourselves slip like that. It's everyone's best interest that we nurture a healthy self-love.

We have to learn to be comfortable with the label of being No.1 in our lives. None of this "Oh I couldn't possibly be that."

You are. You always have been. You just forgot. Now it's time to remember.

AFFIRMATIONS

- ❑ I choose to feel good about myself
- ❑ I am worthy of my own love
- ❑ I enjoy my life to the fullest
- ❑ I am in control of my life
- ❑ Every day and in every way I'm getting better and better
- ❑ Nobody is in control of my life but me
- ❑ I am proud of me
- ❑ I love who I am
- ❑ I love who I am, I am safe and secure
- ❑ I am beautiful, powerful and successful
- ❑ I have the self-esteem, power and confidence to move forwards in my life
- ❑ I need no one's approval but my own
- ❑ I deeply love and respect myself

MEDITATION

1. Identify you're issues and/or problems in terms of a lack of self esteem due to popular culture pressures that you want to heal.
2. Find your quiet space and time.
3. Put on your meditation music and ask for healing from your "source" in terms of your issues and/or problems.
4. Relax, focus on your breath and allow yourself to drift away to a place of total relaxation, release and healing.

A few crystals that would be ideal to be used during this meditation or, indeed, to carry around in regards to issues derived from a lack of self-esteem due to popular culture pressures are:

Citrine: (Yellow Quartz. Colour can also range from lemon-yellow to smoky gold) Citrine helps to raise self-esteem levels and helps to synthesize your understanding when you feel you are being pulled in many directions.

Erythrite: (brilliant pink/red which looks like a velvety covering on its host rock) Erythrite teaches self-love and love of others. It speeds up the path to self love and self acceptance.

Iolite: (Iolite is the gem trade name for the translucent blue and violet cordierite) Connecting with your soul through iolite brings a total state of unconditional self-love.

Charoite: (Ranges from brilliant purple to duller purple to pink. Usually found as a form of masses and tiny crystal druse on host rock) Charoite enhances self-esteem, intuition and assists in bringing about a relaxing, meditative state.

The citrine crystal is best placed on the navel or solar plexus chakra for best results. Erythrite is best on the heart chakra. Iolite is best placed on the third eye and crown chakra's and chariote is best on the third eye.

VISUALIZATION

Five minutes, that's all it takes. Just find your five minutes a few times during your days and nights, quiet the mind, still the body and see yourself with a very healthy self-esteem. Visualize yourself walking, standing, talking, acting and feeling totally confident about who you are. If you feel nervous around certain people, if you feel, deep down, that you've given your power up to these people in the past, then reverse it. See yourself with those very people and see yourself sitting in your power, feeling very comfortable and powerful around them.

Before you can actually assume a carriage of self-confidence it's absolutely essential that you see it first. Your affirmations are also a major part and the meditations too, but visualizing yourself full of self-love and totally comfortable with your new found power is the technique that will make it real for you. So get to it. There's no time to waste. Your new, powerful, wonderful and happy life awaits you.

Come to the edge, he said.
They said: we are afraid.
Come to the edge, he said.
They came,
He pushed them...and they flew.

GUILLAUME APOLLINAIRE

ACHIEVEMENT

A LACK OF SELF WORTH THWARTS our achievements constantly. We all need to know that everything we ever wanted to do, we can do! Nothing is impossible. Only our lack of self-esteem, which manifests into doubts, blocks and fears, stops us. We fall into safety-zones of complacency that take a huge amount of energy to break away from.

If you wanted to be a movie star, pop star, rocket scientist, doctor, nurse, mother, father, bus driver, sports star, politician, or anything at all, you can. It only takes one decision and then the work necessary to achieve any of the above. For instance, let's say you want to be a recording artist but you've never sung in your life and you're fifty years old. No problem! You make the decision to become a recording artist. You get right behind that decision and believe you can do it. You go and get yourself singing lessons. You research recording artists that work in the area you also want to work in and discover what they do. You learn to act like them, sound like them, look like them and think like them. You find where your niche is in that industry. Where a song from an incredibly groovy fifty year old is going to work. You find the right song, you get the right people behind you and you put it out there in market.

Impossible you say? Hard to believe?... Rubbish! How old is Mick Jagger? He's in his sixties. Rod Stewart is still putting out albums and he's in his fifties. So too is David Bowie, Blondie, Madonna even. For crying out loud, the pop prince himself, Michael Jackson is forty-six years old at time of writing! It's not impossible at all. The only thing that can possibly stop you is you not believing that you can do it. And your not believing you can do it is your self-esteem saying you're not good enough because you don't have enough self-love. You're not "No.1" to you.

George Foreman won the heavy weight championship of the world for the second time when he was forty-five. He's now going back to try and win it again at the age of fifty-five. He simply doesn't accept the idea of age as a barrier. It's just not in his thinking. He has been quoted as saying, "I don't get up in the mornings with aches and pains and feeling like I can't do it. I get up in the mornings feeling great and that I can do anything!" Wow! That's just fantastic. Even if he doesn't win the championship this time around, who the hell is going to blame him for trying? Not me, that's for sure.

I saw two fathers who were training their sons to compete in the iron man competitions. These are grueling surf races consisting of swimming out through the surf and back to the beach, running along the beach, then paddling surf ski's out through the surf and back again and finishing with sprint up the beach. It's exhausting and the athletes need to have great strength and endurance. These two fathers were in their fifties and, whilst training their respective sons, they got so fit themselves they decided to compete as well.

In my local cricket association there are a few men still playing who are in their fifties, sixties and even seventies! These men are inspirations.

If all these so called "oldies" can be so active and productive then there really is no excuse for anyone any younger than them for not "having a go" and getting out there and achieving. The only thing stopping anyone from achieving anything they want in their lives is the fact that you don't believe you deserve it because you have low self-worth.

It's important to realize that all of the people you hold in awe such as movie stars, pop stars, presidents and politicians, TV stars, writers, sports hero's, Olympians, and so on, are all people just like you. They are no different to you. They were born and, in most cases, grew up in a household like you.

They went to school, played sport, had friends, did homework, got into trouble with teachers and mum and dad and all the rest of the things that happen to "normal, ordinary people". **They are simply ordinary people doing extraordinary things.** Why? Because they believe they can. That's all. They believe in themselves. They feel they are worthy of success and achievement and they decide to chase whatever dream they want and then they put in all the work necessary to achieve those dreams. Some, however, are not happy. Even with all of the trappings that come with success. Some people become driven by the lure of ego gratification. This is not the reason for seeking achievement. Just achieving is the reward in itself.

The perfect mix for success and happiness is to have

healthy doses of self-worth and self-love. You can feel worthy without having self-love however the mixture of the two is crucial to a balanced, successful and happy life. So you see, you too can be an ordinary person doing extraordinary things. You simply have to choose to be, feel worthy and self-loved, do the work required and achieve whatever it is you want to achieve. No one can stop you but yourself!

AFFIRMATIONS

- ❑ I can do anything I want to do
- ❑ I will never be defeated by anyone or anything
- ❑ I am the greatest!
- ❑ I'm not afraid of anyone or anything
- ❑ I am powerful, confident and successful
- ❑ Nothing will stop me from being a success
- ❑ No one can stop me from being a success
- ❑ I love being successful
- ❑ I never give up
- ❑ I deserve nothing but the best
- ❑ My goals are my right
- ❑ I am successful every single day in every single way
- ❑ I am a winner
- ❑ Today is the first day of the rest of my life
- ❑ My world is what I make of it
- ❑ I believe in me. I am worthy

MEDITATION

1. Identify your issues and/or problems in terms of a lack of drive towards achievement due to a lack of self-worth that you want to heal.
2. Find your quiet space and time.
3. Put on your meditation music and ask for healing from your "source" in terms of your issues and/or problems.
4. Relax, focus on your breath and allow yourself to drift away to a place of total relaxation, release and healing.

A few crystals that would be ideal to be used during this meditation or, indeed, to carry around in regard to issues derived from a lack of drive towards achievement due to a lack of self-worth are:

Blue Tourmaline (Indicolite):
(Blue) Helps in decision making when you are feeling in conflict about which path to take. Focuses personal power and helps you point it in the right direction.

Unakite: (A composite of orange/pink epidote and quartz which occurs in massive form) Unakite enhances self-esteem and feelings of self-worth, and also enhances your sense of personal power.

Amazonite: (Opaque, blue-green feldspar) Amazonite is excellent for enhancing creative expression and gives a clear vision of your harmful tendencies, making then easier to release. It also is excellent for building self confidence and self-esteem and a belief in oneself.

Blue Tourmaline is best placed on the throat and third eye chakra's. Amazonite is Is best placed on the throat chakra and Unakite is best placed on the heart and Solar plexus chakra's.

VISUALIZATION

It is crucial with any form of achievement that you visualize it first. Olympic runners do it constantly. Especially the 100 metre runners. They will go over the race in their heads before they run it. They will see how they run, stride for stride. Other athletes and sports people use visualization also. It's pretty well common practice in this day and age. So it makes perfect sense for you to use it right now in you life.

Decide on whatever it is that you want to achieve and, take five minutes anytime during the day or night, find a quiet spot and still the mind and the body and then see yourself already achieving that thing you're striving for. See it clearly and distinctly as if it were right here, right now. I cannot stress enough how essential this technique is in terms of achievement. It's crucial. So if you want something, then go out and get it. But don't forget to see yourself as already having it first.

There is but one cause,
Of human failure,
And that is
Man's lack of faith
In his true self

WILLIAM JAMES

STRESS!

STRESS KILLS. THERE'S NO DOUBT ABOUT IT. We all know that. It's fact and it's been proven now over and over again. Overloads of stress and long term stress can cause terminal dis-ease within the body. People can, and do, lose their lives due to this kind of stress.

But what is this thing called stress? Where does it come from? Who invented it? How do we get stressed? A popular myth is that we need to have a stressful nature in the first place in order to take on stress. However that's not totally true. It is true that, at times, we all experience stress in our mind and bodies. That's because stress is created by conflict, by being overwhelmed, by feelings of hopelessness, of not coping with responsibility and more.

The common denominator in all of those feelings is a serious lack of self-love. Deep, deep down in our sub-conscious we really do know that we're worthy. We do know we deserve to be No.1. Everyday, however, everything impacts on our mind, body and soul to tell us this isn't so. "No way! We're not worthy of self-love at all". This creates conflict. When we feel overwhelmed by all of our stressful situations that too is a lack of self-love. Our lack of self-esteem is saying we're not good enough to cope with life and we may as well give up. If we feel hopeless, again, we don't give ourselves the credit that we can handle anything. The same goes for responsibility. We're not worthy of responsibility. What were we thinking when we took it on?

The truth is that we can eliminate all stress from our mind, body and soul by finding our true self-worth and self-love. If we unconditionally love ourselves then we can take on any situation and cope admirably. Nothing will get us down. Why should it? We can cope. We believe in ourselves. We don't need any White Knights to come along and alleviate our stressful situations. We can handle it ourselves. We're taking responsibility for ourselves as well. We are stress-free and liberated. This increases our sense of well being mentally, emotionally and physically.

Taking responsibility for all of our actions and words is another way of getting rid of stress from our lives. As I've already said, taking responsibility for ourselves also allows others to take responsibility for themselves. This is totally liberating and freeing. You can't be stressed if you're not taking on any guilt. Guilt doesn't exist. If you take on guilt you're saying, in effect, that no one can make mistakes. This is playing God and won't do at all! Of course we can make mistakes. That's how we learn for crying out loud. We take responsibility for our mistakes, learn from them, and then move on, positively in our lives.

Boris Becker, the champion tennis player from Germany,

was once knocked out of a major tournament, very early, by a lowly ranked player. The media throng was aghast that such a champion as Boris Becker could have something like this happen to him. They were quite agitated and upset by the whole thing. He noticed this and he stopped them and simply stated, "Look, nobody died and there wasn't a war"! In other words, get over it, it's a tennis game after all, I'll learn from my mistakes today and move on and hopefully be better in my next tournament.

This is also a lesson for you to listen to people. There are philosophers in all walks of life. Who would've thought that a professional tennis player could be so positive and wise? Even children can come up with some of the most innocent and truthful wisdom's you've ever heard. They see things so clearly and in an untainted way and can often cut through all the added "junk" we grown ups can dump on a situation and come up with a solution bereft of any stress and worry. So be alert and listen. You never know what you might hear.

AFFIRMATIONS

- ❑ I am safe from the pressures others sometimes place on me
- ❑ I can handle anything life throws at me
- ❑ I am in control of my life
- ❑ I love and forgive myself
- ❑ I live in harmony with others
- ❑ I am responsible for my life
- ❑ I am calm, relaxed and confident
- ❑ I am safe and secure
- ❑ There is nothing worth worrying about
- ❑ Everything happens for a reason
- ❑ I don't judge others
- ❑ I don't allow anyone to judge me
- ❑ I never doubt myself
- ❑ I let go of all guilt
- ❑ I release all my fears
- ❑ I feel the fear and do it anyway
- ❑ I love and learn from all of my mistakes

MEDITATION

1. Identify your issues and/or problems in terms of stress due to a lack of self-worth that you want to heal.
2. Find your quiet space and time.
3. Put on your meditation music and ask for healing from your "source" in terms of your issues and/or problems.
4. Relax, focus on your breath and allow yourself to drift away to a place of total relaxation, release and healing.

A few crystals that would be ideal to be used during this meditation or, indeed, to carry around in regard to issues concerning stress due to a lack of self-worth are:

Amethyst: (Ranges from lavender to violet to almost black) Amethyst has a calming mental effect and is one of the best stones used for meditation. It's particularly useful for overworked, overstressed and overwhelmed mental states.

Ametrine: (A combination of amethyst and citrine) Ametrine provides for clearer insight and ease of decision making. It relieves stress and tension and provides a calming effect.

Smithsonite: (Light blue, light green, yellowish, pink and lavender) Smithsonite brings tranquillity to stressful situations and is soothing and calming. It also assists in physical healing.

Onyx: (A variety of chalcedony) Onyx is a good stone to use as an emotional balancer and to relieve stress and tension. It assists in creativity and inspiration.

Ametrine and Amethyst are best placed on the solar plexus, third eye and crown Chakra's while the smithsonite and Onyx crystals are best placed according to colour but can be generally used on all chakra points.

VISUALIZATION

It's essential to use visualization in regards to issues dealing with stress. If you're stressed then your mind is telling your body you're stressed. To counter that we must first use affirmations, then meditate and then we must see ourselves as stress free.

So find your five minutes each day and night, find a quiet spot, close you eyes, still your mind and body and begin to visualize your stress-free world. See yourself in a situation where previously you've not coped well and taken on stress, then see yourself coping brilliantly and taking on no stress whatsoever.

If you've had situations where you've felt under pressure and felt stressed about that then see yourself, very clearly, in those situations right now, dealing with them easily and comfortably and without stress. You must visualize yourself with these new attitudes and feelings as if you have them right now this very minute! Don't see it happening in the future. Your sub-conscious mind is a very literal one and will take that as a sign that you don't need those new feelings and attitudes yet. They're to come as it were, and your sub-conscious will always have those feelings and attitudes "pending". You'll always be waiting for them. This is the reason, for all visualizations, that you must see whatever it is you're working on in the "now". Right here and right now. Not tomorrow because, in that case, tomorrow will never come.

The snow goose,
Need not bathe,
To make itself white.
Neither can you,
Do anything,
But be yourself

LAO-TSE

THE FAÇADE

THE EPITOME OF SELF-LOATHING in our present culture is cosmetic plastic surgery. I will fight for everybody's right to freedom of choice. So long as everyone knows exactly why they're making those choices. They need to know all the facts. All the probable results and the real reasons for those choices. The obvious question in relation to plastic surgery is "why are you changing your appearance?" If it's not because you've been horribly maimed in an accident, then why? The obvious answer is that you're not happy with how you look. Why is that? Is there a list somewhere, a chart, a decree that states how everyone should look and if you don't fit the bill then you'd better change? I don't think there is. I've never seen or heard of one. So I don't really think that such a quality control system is really in place.

What's really wrong with small breasts, prominent noses, thin lips, wrinkles, flabby tummies, cellulite, and so on, and so on? Who decided that these things needed changing in people?

Was it a God or something? I'm sorry but I just don't get it. If you have self-love, if you deem yourself worthy, why on earth would you let a man or a woman with a scalpel and a vacuum cleaner cut you open and suck away parts of your body? Or cut your face up and put staples in your skin and take way part of your nose, your chin, or your breasts? Why would you let a plastic surgeon cut your breasts open and shove a man-made substance in there forever, just so you can wear a bigger bra? Again, I'm not arguing against anyone's freedom of choice to do anything they want to their face or bodies. That's any individual's choice. I'm simply asking the question as to why one would make some of these cosmetic decisions if one has self-love.

If you have unconditional self-love you will look in the mirror and see beauty. Every single day. No matter what shape or size you are. No matter whether you've got wrinkles or a big nose. And do you know what? Everybody else will see it the same way!

To attract the people and "things" we want in our life we don't need to cut ourselves up and change the outside of us. We need only look inside of us and find the love.

There are many valid ways of changing our appearance that can be positive for our self-esteem and our mind, body and soul all at the same time. Exercise! Running, swimming, gym, individual and team sports, are all good activities which allow us to exercise our bodies and our minds. We can achieve exercise goals. We can also exercise our self-worth to perform well at the same time.

All the while we can keep our bodies in good health and shape. Whatever that shape may be. If you're a bigger person, be a happy bigger person. If you're a smaller person then be a happy smaller person. Who says you can't? If you feel you're overweight and want to be thinner then decide to lose weight, adjust your diet accordingly and then get out there and exercise. If you feel you're too thin and you want to beef it up a bit, then adjust your diet accordingly and get out there and exercise as well. Strengthen your body. Put on muscle. You'll feel good *because* you'll look good, and you'll look good, because you'll feel good. It's a self-fulfilling prophecy. It's nothing but a "win, win" situation. You cannot lose if you love yourself enough to make positive changes to your diet and exercise regimes.

Your self-worth is your only true measure. Nothing else. No magazines or TV shows. They don't work. Even super models aren't happy with the way they look. When will we see someone with the absolutely "perfect look"? Even then, will they be happy? Where does it end? Well it's got to stop somewhere, and that somewhere is with you. Look inside. There's perfection inside all of us!

AFFIRMATIONS

- ❑ Changing my mind, changes my body and changing my body, changes my mind
- ❑ I love me just the way I am
- ❑ (Say this one into the mirror in the morning and at night. At least!) I love me (insert your name) and I love my beauty and my body.
- ❑ My true beauty dwells deep within me
- ❑ I feel good about myself
- ❑ I am at home with who I am
- ❑ My beauty shines out from within
- ❑ I am always loved for who I am
- ❑ I am unique and wonderful
- ❑ No matter what people think of me I always feel good about my self
- ❑ I look after my body and my mind
- ❑ I love my body and only feed it healthy food
- ❑ I love my mind and only feed it healthy thoughts
- ❑ I respect myself and only make healthy choices in my life
- ❑ I am grateful for a healthy body
- ❑ I love my life and I love me

MEDITATION

1. Identify your issues and/or problems in terms of how you look, or how you think you should look, that you want to heal.
2. Find your quiet space and time.
3. Put on your meditation music and ask for healing from your "source" in terms of your issues and/or problems.
4. Relax, focus on your breath and allow yourself to drift away to a place of total relaxation, release and healing.

A few crystals that would be ideal to be used during this meditation or, indeed, to carry around in regard to issues concerning your façade are:

Marcasite: (Black with streaks of marcasite appearing as goldish swirls) This stone will help surround you with a protective field and leave you feeling calmer and more able to express the true you

Chariote: (Ranges from brilliant purple to duller purple and to pink) Assists in clearing emotional and mental blocks which prevent you from changing your attitude. Enhances self-esteem.

Blue Aventurine:

(Blue) Blue aventurine assists in breaking down belief systems that prevent you from taking the most beneficial path open to you. Gives you belief and aids your ability to make correct decisions

Red Quartz: (Red) This stone cuts through negativity. It helps you to enjoy life just as it is. It dissipates greed, jealousy and envy and helps you to be satisfied with what you have right now

The marcasite crystal is best placed on the crown and the base or root chakra's.

Blue aventurine is best on the third eye chakra. Red Quartz is best on the base or Root chakra and chariote is best on the third eye chakra.

VISUALIZATION

Now this is an important area of your life with which to use visualization. If we want to change the way we look for whatever reason, bigger or smaller, beefier or more lithe, stronger or less defined, we MUST first see ourselves with that body we want. If you see it clearly in your mind's eye, and believe it, then you will have it.

I have done this myself. I wanted to be stronger, more muscular with better posture. (I was a little stooped or round-shouldered). So I simply started visualizing myself the way I wanted to look. I was inspired from attending a course to join a gym. I'd previously been hopeless with regular gym attendance all my life. I always stopped going after an initial burst of energy. However, this time I stuck. I also changed my diet, gave up alcohol and played competitive sport again. All the while I saw the new body I wanted to have.

I ended up with that body shape and maintain it to this day. This was a body shape I thought was never the body shape for me. Never in a million years did I think I could achieve something like that. But I did. I'm healthier and fitter and am in the best shape of my life now in my forties.

I've even witnessed a woman whose breasts grew simply through the use of visualization. She didn't go from an "A" cup to a "DD" cup but her breasts did grow to a size she was very happy with. In her visualization she saw herself with the size she wanted and she now has them. This is pretty amazing stuff and just goes to show you the power of your mind and your sub-conscious. Never be misguided into thinking we're playing with funny little magical games here. This is powerful, quantifiable stuff.

So, find your five minutes alone during your days or nights and sit still and see the body you want. See yourself as having that body RIGHT NOW! Keep it up. Don't be disheartened if there's not a lot of movement right away. Be patient and be persistent. Nothing comes without a bit of work. But you're worth the hard work, isn't that right? Yes, that's right. So go to it. The new you is only an image in your mind away.

A tree that can fill the span
Of a man's arms
Grows from a downy tip;
A terrace nine storeys high
Rises from hodfuls of earth;
A journey of a thousand miles
Starts from beneath one's feet.

LAO-TZU

PARENTING

OUR PARENTS HAVE A HUGE EFFECT on our self-esteem and on how we see ourselves as individuals. Our sense of identity is tied up with who our parents are and how they brought us up. A lot of the time even the best of parents make mistakes which impinge upon a positive upbringing of any child. The danger is to blame parents for these mistakes. By blaming our parents for everything simply makes an offender out of them and, worse, a victim out of us. Taking on victim-hood promotes an incredible lack of self-esteem. It places blame firmly and decisively elsewhere which conveniently alleviates us from taking any responsibility for where we are in our lives at any given moment.

We need to forgive our parents for the mistakes they've made. We need to take responsibility ourselves for how we feel and act and move on in life with a positive outlook. All parents make mistakes. Our parents made mistakes. Their parents made mistakes and we as parents will make mistakes as well.

Most of the time the mistakes made have been, or will be, because of love.

There is no such thing as the "perfect parent". There is no university or college we can go to and earn a degree or diploma in "parent-hood" either. The rules are passed down through the ages. Old mistakes are remedied by one generation who swear "not to make the same mistakes my parents made"! Only to be replaced by new mistakes by the current generation. Personally, I feel I'm one of the best parents I've ever seen and I know for a fact I'm making mistakes all the time. It can't be helped. So let's take the heat off parents and take control of our own world for once.

The bottom line with parenting is to give our children unconditional love, foster a healthy self-love/self-esteem within them and treat them with respect. Discipline is a major factor in child-rearing too. Children see appropriate discipline as caring. As Love. We berate our young children for crossing the road without a parent because we're frightened for their safety. They recognize that and wouldn't have it any other way.

This also fosters self-worth as they see that if their parents care about them then they must be worth something. Too much freedom for young children lowers their self-esteem. If mum and dad let their child run around the neighbourhood until all hours then that child will feel unloved, un-cared for, worthless. They then tend to "act up" so as to be disciplined/cared for. You know the one where the teenage daughter says "Mum, dad please let me go to the party with all my friends?" You aren't satisfied that the party is a safe one and so you say no.

She becomes incredibly upset and tells you exactly what

she thinks of you and how you are "ruining her life" before collapsing in tears in her room. What she is really saying is "Thank you so much mum and dad. I didn't really like the people holding the party and I knew that some people going were a little scary but my friends were all going and I had to find a way to get out of it. Thank goodness you care about me and stopped me!"

No doubt there'll be the occasion where you stop your fourteen-year-old daughter from going to the really "hot" and perfectly safe party! But how could you know? You can only go with your gut instincts and try and protect your child. Oh well, there goes a mistake you just made as a parent. See, some of the mistakes are made with the best of intentions. The fourteen-year-old can't blame you twenty years later for being the reason she's isolationist and shy. She has to work on her own issues of low self-esteem to deal with that. Taking a victim stance and blaming others will not get her anywhere. She'll need to take responsibility for her situation before she can move on. Just as we have to in relation to all the mistakes our parents have made with us. They are not to blame. They were just doing their job. And for the most part, probably doing a pretty good job at that.

There is a slightly different healing path one needs to travel in terms of cruel and abusive parents. If there has been long-term mental and emotional abuse or sexual abuse then these are much stronger issues than the rather "normal" parenting mistakes I've mentioned thus far. However, in terms of anyone moving on from an abusive past or from issues relating to "normal" parenting mistakes, the healing methods are relatively the same.

Forgiveness is the key to all of it. Without forgiveness you'll simply go on living with anger, hate, the need for revenge and so on. All of these emotions will do nothing to the parent they're aimed at. They will most probably be totally unaware of your feelings. No, the only thing those stored up negative emotions will do is make you ill. Perhaps even terminally. Allowing them to fester within could very easily cause cancer to grow.

So you need to clear those emotions and the only way to do that is to forgive. This does not mean that you forget. You will never forget any form of serious abuse, but by forgiving you are able to move on, positively in your life. When you see that abusive parent you can confront him or her. Tell them what they have done to you, how they have affected your life. Then you can tell them that you forgive them so that you can be free of them for once and for all. You will find that you will be totally liberated by taking this course of action.

AFFIRMATIONS

- ❑ I take full responsibility for my own life
- ❑ I create my own reality
- ❑ My issues are my own
- ❑ I trust myself
- ❑ Old negative patterns do not serve me. I let them go
- ❑ I am my own person
- ❑ My mistakes are my own. I learn from them and move on
- ❑ I let love and understanding flow through me
- ❑ I respect myself and all others
- ❑ My world is what I want it to be
- ❑ I choose to be free and safe
- ❑ I am worthy if giving and receiving unconditional love
- ❑ My world is of my own making
- ❑ Living a responsible life is easy for me.

MEDITATION

1. Identify your issues and/or problems in terms of parenting that you want to heal.
2. Find your quiet space and time.
3. Put on your meditation music and ask for healing from your "source" in terms of your issues and/or problems.
4. Relax, focus on your breath and allow yourself to drift away to a place of total relaxation, release and healing.

A few crystals that would be ideal to be used during this meditation or, indeed, to carry around in regard to issues concerning parenting are:

Green Apatite: (Yellow and yellow/green) This crystal is comforting and inward looking. It enhances unconditional love towards others and self-empowerment and self-esteem

Unakite: (Orange/pink feldspar, epidote and quartz) This crystal encourages you to be more forthright about your needs and desires and to be more confident about what you want in life. It transmutes worthlessness to worthiness, self-hatred to self-love, self-doubt to confidence and belief in your power and ability

Brown Barite: (Brown) Brown Barite works quickly to dissolve feelings of disquiet and concern about situations that are not of your doing. Its message is "live and let live". Clears unwanted and lingering negative energies and soothes old angers

Clear Flourite: (Clear) Clear Flourite helps focus your attention on the present moment and free yourself from the hold of the past.

The apatite and Unakite crystals are best placed on the heart and solar plexus Chakra's. Brown barite is best placed on the base or root chakra and clear flourite is best on the third eye and crown chakra's.

VISUALIZATION

If you have issues with either of your parents and feel that there is unfinished business in terms of your relationship with them then visualization is very important. A brilliant start to dealing with those issues is to see yourself with that parent, right now, without those very issues being involved.

In other words, you need to be free of all blame, angst, anger or whatever in regards to your parents. This is the same for "normal" parenting mistakes and for abusive parents too.

So, find your five minutes, find a quiet place where you won't be interrupted, still the mind and body and begin your visualization. See yourself with your parents and see yourself in a totally empowered, unencumbered state. Free from blame and angst. If you had abusive parents, see yourself in control. They no longer have power over you. Whatever power they had, banish it with forgiveness. See yourself free of them and standing there completely powerful.

For parents, see yourself parenting your own children without worrying about all the mistakes you will make. See yourself totally relaxed in your parenting with that relaxed sense being visited upon your children. They will benefit a great deal as you heal yourself.

If you do,
What you've always done,
You'll get,
What you've always gotten.

UNKNOWN

LANGUAGE

LANGUAGE IS SO IMPORTANT. What we say and how we say it goes a long way to affecting our sense of self-esteem. Our words are just the logical extension of our thoughts. So, to a large extent, what we're saying is what we're thinking. If we say something negative about one particular area of our lives then that negative comment will pervade all of our experiences. Saying things like, "I'm no good at that," I can't do it," "I've never been any good at doing that," "Oh, I'm hopeless," "I never get it right," "I can't play that game," "I'm not funny" or "I'm not smart enough," only explains our attitudes about ourselves. And those are bad attitudes. All these phrases are what I call "self-esteem sabotage". They simply reinforce the fact that we think we're not good enough. That simply isn't true but we'll keep believing it if we keep on saying it.

If we're not particularly proficient at a sport, game, profession or whatever, it's because we haven't chosen to be so in the first place. Those things have not been in our life's experience to this point. I'm not a rocket scientist because that area has never interested me. It's not because I'm not good enough to be one. Without the interest I didn't go down a path of study that would've put me in a position to become a rocket scientist. Simple.

However, I would've loved to have been a professional footballer (Australian Rules). So why aren't I? I'm not one because I didn't think in my earlier years, deep down, that I was good enough to be one. That thought created negative language about me and football and it was those thoughts and that language that stopped me. If I'd seriously considered myself worthy of being a professional footballer I would have made the decision to be one and I would've worked hard at the training and played the game and never given up until I made it. And I would've made it. I don't doubt that for a minute.

However, I constantly used language that came from my deep sub-conscious that let me know I couldn't be a professional footballer. Language such as "I'm too light," "I can't jump high enough," I'm not strong enough," "I'm too skinny," "I'm too scared of getting hurt," "football is only for those big tough guys" and so on. The truth is that I could have over come all of those doubts even if they were true but my constant negative language told me not to bother as I was "not good enough."

All of my life I have been interested in martial arts. I love the action movies and always looked enviously at people walking from their martial arts classes with their white uniforms on and their many coloured belts. Obviously the belt I envied most was the black one. If someone mentioned to me that a person they knew was a black belt in a martial art I would immediately be in awe of that person. When I would meet them I'd treat them with the respect I thought they deserved for being a black belt.

Obviously being a black belt myself in a martial art was impossible. My negative self-talk always said, "No man, that's not for you. That's for all those tough martial arts kinda guys." "You're not one of them. Don't even think of going there. It won't happen. Forget about it!" My language reflected this self-talk and was always negative in regards to any perceived notion I might have had to participate in a martial art. This went on for all of my life until I was 43. By this stage I had done a lot of work on myself. I had done a lot of healing, meditation and affirmations. I also had a lot more positive self-talk going on. Suddenly my two young sons decided to take up Taekwondo. So I took them along and watched thinking maybe I can live my martial arts dream, vicariously, through them. They progressed from the initial white belt to the yellow belt, with the eldest progressing to the next blue belt. After watching for a while I got the idea that this could actually be for me. The scars from the years and years of negative self-talk were still there and were creating a lot of nervousness. Thankfully my new positive self won out and I began Taekwondo as a novice white belt. Well I loved it and I worked my butt off! I graded up to a new belt every time there was a grading day. I learnt the patterns, I learnt the kicks, the sparring, the board breaking and so on. Not only that, but the whole philosophy of Taekwondo is actually against violence, so it sat brilliantly with my own take on life. It teaches you how *not* to fight. The actual Taekwondo credo is to get the whole world participating and then there'll be no more war. That's a cool credo!

Well anyway, guess what? Yes that's right, I achieved a black belt in Taekwondo! After all these years. And, yes, it feels great! Now you have to remember that my negative self-talk was *so* strong on this. Having a black belt in a martial art was just *not* in my realm of reality. But now I have one and I *am* one. For me this is a huge breakthrough and my black belt proves to me, every day, the power of positive self-talk and language. It's just *so* important.

We need to be diligent, vigilant and persistent in our appraisal of the language we use. We need to pick ourselves up on our negative language, and others too, and change the negatives into positives. We need to use phrases such as "I haven't experienced that yet" or "That's not been my experience to this point," instead of "I can't do that." "I need to practice some more and I'll be good at that," "I haven't chosen to do that," It's not something that's taken my interest," or "I can do it if I really set my mind to it," instead of "I'm hopeless at that" and so on. These phrases send positive messages to your sub-conscious and empower you. You know you can do anything if you truly want to. If you haven't yet then there are reasons, but the reason is never because you're "not good enough." That phrase is hereby banished from your vocabulary. It doesn't exist any longer. You are always good enough. You have simply chosen, or not chosen, to take certain paths in life. It's simply choice. No judgment. Just choice.

Obviously using negative language has a huge effect on our self-worth. When we say we're no good at something we're putting ourselves down and saying we're actually not worthy. I couldn't be a professional footballer because I wasn't worthy of being one, in my mind. Our self-worth is incredibly important in every area in our life. We must use language that supports our self-worth, how we value ourselves. No more self put-downs! No more self sabotage! If you can't speak kindly about yourself, then who can? Make note from this moment on how you use language in relation to yourself. Concentrate on what you say and notice how often you speak negatively about yourself. Let a partner, lover, close friend, family member or whatever, know about the language issue and have them monitor your language and you monitor theirs. Pick each other up on your negative speak. You'll be amazed at how often you do it without even knowing its been going on. Notice then how your attitude towards yourself changes and then notice how your whole life changes *because* of that attitude change. You will be positively amazed.

What we say affects others also. Positive phrases and statements tend to rub off on people around you. As will the negative ones! Especially children that see you as a role model. And, really, what children don't see any adult as a role model. Children look to everyone older then them to show them the way in this weird and wacky world they've been born into.

So this is another important reason for vigilance and awareness of what we say about ourselves. Everything grows in an exponential manner in terms of influence. So that if we're always positive about ourselves others will pick up on that and be more inclined to be positive about themselves and will act in a positive manner to even more people. Those people will be more inclined to be positive about themselves and to others around *even more* people and so it grows. The responsibility to be positive is great. We can help to change the world just by the way we think and speak about ourselves and others. So don't let the team down OK?

AFFIRMATIONS

- ❑ I am what I say I am
- ❑ I only ever speak my truth
- ❑ I am worthy of praise
- ❑ I choose to say only good things about myself and others
- ❑ My life is rich. I can do anything
- ❑ I am a wonderful person.
- ❑ What I think is what I say and I think I'm great!
- ❑ What I focus on increases so I only focus on good things
- ❑ I am in control of my thoughts, feelings and language
- ❑ I am what I think I am
- ❑ I only ever speak kindly of myself
- ❑ I love me and I tell myself so
- ❑ Talk is cheap, so I can afford to speak well of myself more often
- ❑ I was born positive
- ❑ I love my life and I let myself know
- ❑ My words are in good hands
- ❑ Love pervades my thoughts, words and actions

MEDITATION

1. Identify your issues and/or problems in terms of language, of how you speak about yourself and about others that you want to heal.
2. Find your quiet space and time.
3. Put on your meditation music and ask for healing from your "source" in terms of your issues and/or problems.
4. Relax, focus on your breath and allow yourself to drift away to a place of total relaxation, release and healing.

A few crystals that would be ideal to be used during this meditation or to carry around regard to issues concerning how we think about ourselves and therefore the language we use in relation to ourselves are:

Amazonite: (Opaque, blue-green feldspar) Amazonite helps to give a clear vision of your harmful tendencies, making them easier to release. Also excellent for building self-esteem and a belief in yourself.

Sodalite: (Bright blue. Often crisscrossed with white and grey lines) Sodalite helps to clear old mental patterns from the sub-conscious to make way for conscious thinking. It brings clarity and enhances communication.

White Coral: (White) This organic gem strengthens your self-esteem and assists with clear judgment.

It also encourages you to affirm yourself and recognize the self within.

Chrysocolla: (Opaque, blue-green hydrous copper silicate) Chrysocolla enhances creative expression, power and communication. It also helps to clear links with the past as you move forward.

All of these crystals are best placed on the throat chakra. The throat chakra is all about self-expression, communication, speaking your truth etc. However Chrysocolla and sodalite can also be placed on the third eye and heart chakras as well.

VISUALIZATION

An obvious first step to changing your opinion about yourself and, therefore, your language in relation to yourself is to see yourself with this new attitude. You will need to find your five minutes of quiet, anytime during the day or night, where you can be still with a quiet mind and begin to visualize yourself with this new attitude that is going to inform your language which will, in turn, reinforce your new attitude.

Again, it's a wonderfully positive cycle that supports itself. You need to see yourself clearly, in the now, with a new positive attitude that only brings about positive reinforcement. Where you used to put yourself down, you don't anymore. You only speak kindly about yourself.

Visualizing this way will also become a great tool in monitoring your negative speak. You'll become much more aware of how you speak negatively about yourself once you see yourself in a more positive way.

Perfect kindness,
Acts,
Without thinking,
Of kindness

LAO-TSE

ABUSE

ONE OF THE GREATEST REASONS for someone to lose their self-esteem, to stop loving themselves, is for that person to become the victim of abuse. All abuse causes our self-worth to tumble and fall to drastically low proportions. All abuse is about giving up your power or having your power taken away from you. Obviously all abuse is wrong and should never be tolerated at any time or for any reason. If you are being abused or know of anyone being abused then you need to talk about it. You need to tell someone. If at first they don't listen then you tell someone else. If they don't listen then tell another and then another and another and so on until someone LISTENS! Abuse damages everyone. Even the abuser. It's a lose, lose situation and must be made apparent and then dealt with and then the parties involved need to be healed.

There are many, many forms of abuse such as emotional, physical, sexual and mental. These are the most obvious and, nearly always, the most damaging forms of abuse. We all know the damage sexual abuse can cause. Especially in the young. Children are innocent, beautiful creatures. They're on a magnificent journey of discovery. They are sponges for knowledge. They want to know who they are and what their purpose is. To violate their dignity, their sexual innocence and their trust, to take away their power and make them feel guilt, fear and disgust is one of the greatest crimes of all time. However, someone who sexually abuses children is a very damaged person in their own right. Often children who have been abused will go on and complete the cycle and become abusers themselves. This doesn't excuse any abuse. It's just a sad and lamentable fact.

I don't know where all of this abuse has begun but I do know where it can end. I firmly believe that a person who has a healthy dose of self-love will never be able to abuse anyone. How could they? No one who is happy within themselves could go out and consciously hurt another. No one who is full of self-love will let anyone else abuse them. They just wouldn't let it happen. They wouldn't allow anyone to violate their personal space or their physical being because they would feel far too worthy for that.

Therefore the greatest tool of all time in terms of abusers is self-love and self-worth. Using a psychological perspective and dragging up the history of the abusers own abuse, delving into their minds to find some form of "weakness" in there doesn't really achieve anything positive at all. In fact I can only see how that form of "therapy" would have a negative affect on someone who is an abuser. Especially if the reason for their abusing is due to their being abused in the first place.

The only reason to re-visit the history of their own abuse is so that they can forgive their abusers in order for them to move on in their own lives. Carrying anger and hate only hurts the person carrying it, (It will also only help to fuel the need to abuse). It has no affect on the person who caused the anger and hate. They don't know what you're feeling and most of the time they don't care. So an abused person needs to forgive the abuser in order to free themselves of those dis-ease causing feelings and emotions.

This is a liberating exercise. It does not excuse the abuse or the abuser it simply frees the abused. One never forgets but it's best to have those memories with no negative feelings and emotions attached. This is the only way to be able to move on in life. It's an imperative and, as hard as it sounds to be able to achieve, it must be done.

To forgive, to move on and to heal will allow a person to feel self-worth again and to find self-love. A person who works hard to get themselves in a state of self-love can never abuse. It's just not possible.

Other forms of abuse can be very subtle and not seem like "real abuse" on the surface. If, let's say, your partner is a very controlling person for instance. If they have to know where you are at all times, who you are with, how much do you spend and what do you spend it on and so on, then they are abusing you. If you don't have your freedom then what do you have? In this situation you have definitely given up your power to another person. Whenever that happens, that's abuse.

Also, just being taken for granted by partners, lovers, family, friends, work-mates, school-mates, teammates and more is a form of abuse. This can be a very subtle but quite insidious form of abuse. It can take someone a long time to suddenly realize that they're being taken for granted/abused. It can whip up great tides of negative emotion in the abused when this realization occurs. In this situation, if this form of abuse is happening then one's self worth is very low as you feel as though no-one cares about you because they continue to "use" you. It takes a healthy dose of self-worth to stand up for oneself and not allow others to take you for granted.

The bottom line with all of this is that no one should ever allow themselves to be put in a position where they become a victim. Victim mode is easy to get into but very hard to get out of. You give up all of your power when you become a victim and that's a hard place to come back from. Being a victim has many modes ranging from the subtle, taking for granted, type of victim-hood to the more disastrous area of being a victim of serious sexual and/or physical abuse. If you love yourself, unconditionally, then you can never become a victim. It's that simple. If every single person living in the world today totally loved themselves unconditionally, there would be no abuse in any way, shape or form. There'd be no war either. Not a bad state of affairs to aim for is it? Well it starts with you. Love yourself. You cannot give yourself or the world a greater gift than that.

AFFIRMATIONS

- ☐ I am the most powerful person I know. No one has power over me
- ☐ I am special and no one can take that from me
- ☐ I choose to respect myself and others
- ☐ My body is my own
- ☐ I am in control of my thoughts and my body
- ☐ I am a loving, wonderful individual
- ☐ I deserve to love myself. It's my right
- ☐ I was born with pure love inside of me
- ☐ I am strong and powerful and in charge of my life
- ☐ No one can take advantage of me. Not even me
- ☐ I make positive difference every time I love
- ☐ I forgive everyone, even myself
- ☐ You can't touch this
- ☐ The only answer is love, sweet love
- ☐ I deserve to be safe, secure and happy
- ☐ I have a very high opinion of myself and that's OK!
- ☐ I'm the most important person I know

MEDITATION

1. Identify your issues and/or problems in terms of abuse that you want to heal.
2. Find your quiet space and time.
3. Put on your meditation music and ask for healing from your "source" in terms of your issues and/or problems.
4. Relax, focus on your breath and allow yourself to drift away to a place of total relaxation, release and healing.

A few crystals that would be ideal to be used during this meditation or to carry around in regard to issues concerning abuse are:

Rose Quartz: (Pink) The rose quartz crystal is often referred to as the "love crystal". It promotes love, forgiveness and compassion. Helps clear stored anger, resentment, guilt and fear. It also enhances self-confidence.

Unakite: (Orange/pink feldspar, epidote and quartz which occurs in massive form) Unakite enhances self-esteem and self-worth. It transmutes feelings of worthlessness to worthiness, self-hatred to self-love, self-doubt to confidence and belief in your power and ability

Yellow Jasper: (Yellow) Yellow jasper is very good for the easing of feelings of powerlessness and emotional blocks. It also calms and soothes.

Lepidolite: (Appears in the form of masses, mica-like layers and tabular crystals) Lepidolite alleviates stress, anger and self-hatred. It helps promote self-love and love of others.

Rose quartz is best placed on the heart chakra. So too is lepidolite. Unakite can be placed on the heart chakra as well as the solar plexus. Yellow jasper is best placed the solar plexus chakra.

VISUALIZATION

If you are a victim of abuse then visualization is crucial. You need to see the change in order to actually change what's happening in your life. So you will need to grab your five minute breaks and begin to see your new life.

If you have someone abusing you then see yourself, very clearly, being very powerful in relation to them. See yourself stopping them from abusing you. See everyone around you believing you and helping get rid of this abusive person.

See yourself living your life with self-love. See yourself as very powerful in your own right. This will fire up your thoughts which will, in turn, motivate your physical self to take positive action to break out of the victim mentality.

If you are an abuser or have abused in the past then you need to see yourself as a totally loved person. A person with a very healthy dose of self-love. A person who could never contemplate harming another person or taking someone's power away from them.

All in all, everyone should see themselves, in the now, as powerful, loving, forgiving and safe people.

To be what we are,
And to become what,
We are capable,
Of becoming,
Is the only end of life

R L STEVENSON

HIDING AWAY

PEOPLE WITH LOW SELF-ESTEEM hide away from the world. This is not to say that they shut themselves away in a dark house, never letting the light of day enter, like the old woman from Great Expectations. (Although some people do, do this). There are far more subtle ways for people to hide away from others.

It can be through having long hair. Long hair is beautiful, don't get me wrong, it's attached to sexuality and all kinds of wonderful things. But some people use long hair in a negative sense in order to hide their face from the world. They let the hair basically cover their faces, especially from the sides so that no one can see what's going on in there. They have true unworthiness attached, which is telling them not to show their faces.

In another way, and mostly for men, especially young men, the "shaved-head" or very, very short hair cut is a way of hiding away. This look has all the connotations of the military, control and the penal system. Pretty scary stuff really. The most important factor, though, is that the shaved look produces "uniformity" amongst people. Which is just another way of hiding away by not standing out in any way shape or form. You're just one of the crowd. No different from the next person. It's really a very clever trick of fashion that whilst, on the surface, promoting outrageousness and anarchy in regards to appearance, the whole "shaved" look actually produces nothing but meek, sheep-like conformity.

This same trick of fashion can apply in regards to clothing as well. The whole trend towards baggy track-suits, caps, beanie hats and bandannas, is *all* about hiding away from the world. Also all of this clothing has basically been derived from the idea of gang life in the USA. Now these gang members are all groups of totally disaffected fatherless young men with incredibly low self-esteem. It's just another way to hide away from the world. Who knows who you really are and what you really look like underneath a beanie or cap and underneath those incredibly baggy pants and tops? If you have a healthy self-love and self-esteem you'll wear what you like and show yourself to the world quite happily and regardless of what people think.

Another way of hiding away from the world is body fat. A lot of people put on the kilos to hide away from life. This is sadly very true for victims of sexual abuse. This group, unfortunately, is made up mostly of young women. They will put on weight so as to not look as attractive to the abuser. It's basically an instinctive and self-protective reaction.

Others with a low self esteem will eat for comfort, putting on weight, not looking as good as they could, accentuating their low self esteem and, therefore, eating more for comfort. It's a vicious cycle which no high profit, vulture-like diet program is ever going to fix. The only answer to these types of weight problems is a healthy dose of self-esteem. One needs to feel good to want to look good and when one looks good one feels good. It's the same cycle as with putting on weight, just positive and in reverse.

So the idea is not to hide away from life. The idea is to build up our self-esteem and self-love and be proud to show ourselves to the world in any way we choose to.

AFFIRMATIONS

- ❑ I feel good and I look good
- ❑ I love who I am
- ❑ I choose to feel great about myself
- ❑ I am beautiful
- ❑ I never worry what other people think
- ❑ I am calm, relaxed and confident about the way I look
- ❑ I always choose the perfect clothes for me
- ❑ I am happy and content
- ❑ I wear whatever I want to wear
- ❑ I am comfortable being me
- ❑ I love showing everyone who I am
- ❑ I love who I am and I'm happy to show it
- ❑ I am my own person
- ❑ I express who I am without fear

MEDITATION

1. Identify your issues and/or problems in terms of hiding away that you want to heal.
2. Find your quiet space and time.
3. Put on your meditation music and ask for healing from your "source" in terms of your issues and/or problems.
4. Relax, focus on your breath and allow yourself to drift away to a place of total relaxation, release and healing.

A few crystals that would be ideal to be used during this meditation or carry around in regard to issues concerning hiding away are:

Fire Agate: (brown to black with orange and red tints) Fire Agate helps clear blocks on the emotional and physical bodies. Brings clarity and understanding to all situations.

Alexandrite: (greenish to deep purple and red) Alexandrite helps to align the emotional and mental bodies and enhances your ability to find joy in life.

Sugalite: (purple. Also known as luvulite or royal azel) It's a link between the mind and the body. It's an emotional balancer and reduces stress. One of the best stones for sensitive and open people.

Staurolite: (also known as fairy cross. Often found as crystal twins forming a cross) Staurolite is a very grounding crystal and it encourages a less materially based existence.

The Fire Agate and Staurolite crystals are best placed on the root or base chakra.

Alexandrite is best on the crown chakra and the Sugalite is best placed on the third eye or crown chakras.

VISUALIZATION

If you feel that you're a person that tends to "hide-away" from people and life in general then visualization is a must for you. So, again, find your five minutes and allow your body and mind to be still. Then begin to see yourself proudly showing yourself to the world. See it happening right now. Not tomorrow or the next day or the next. Right now.

If you've been hiding behind your hair then see yourself with a new haircut that shows your face to the world. See yourself enjoying this and smiling and being happy about it all. If you've been using weight to hide away then see yourself showing your new slimmer body (that's occurred due to positive eating habits and exercise. Not some "miracle diet") to the world with confidence, happiness and joy attached.

If you've been a person who hides away by being just like every one else, by hiding in the mire of anonymity, then you need to see yourself with your own "individual" look that you're proud of. Which singles you out from the crowd. Remember, you are unique. There is no one else like you. Revel in that. Enjoy that. See that in the now. Happening right now. For then it *will* happen.

There is one thing stronger
Than all the armies
Of the world
And that is an idea
Whose time has come.

VICTOR HUGO

KNOWLEDGE

HOW MANY PEOPLE WENT THROUGH their entire school life feeling that they weren't one of the smartest people at their school? I'll take an educated guess and say that most of you reading this book will have said yes to that last question. I know I did. I went through to my early twenties, even into my thirties, thinking I was not the pointiest cue in the rack. At the schools I went to, high academic achievement was everything. If you didn't attain really good marks then you weren't "good enough". Sporting prowess had some merit but was never seen as important as academic success.

Not feeling smart has a huge affect on how you feel about yourself. It can do nothing but promote low self-esteem. The problem is that it's all a complete and utter fallacy. Being academically brilliant has got NOTHING to do with being smart or not. I have known university professors who are, in some situations, among the dumbest people I've ever met. There are so many more areas in life that require varying degrees of intellect than just academia. Retention of knowledge is a skill that can be learnt by anyone. For instance, an IQ test, in fact, only measures how well a person does that specific IQ test. Nothing else! IQ tests have absolutely no relevance in any area of our lives whatsoever. But they are widely regarded as an indicator of how intelligent someone is. This is just plainly ridiculous. I remember reading a book and the author wrote about when he completed a literary IQ test and failed a section on one particular book. He was told that he didn't completely understand the author's intent. It turned out that he *was* the author of the book being used in the test! Enough said.

It takes five to six years of study to become a medical doctor. Doctors know they are going to have to cram and inordinate amount of facts into their heads during that time. They need to retain that information so that when a sick person comes to see them one day, they have inside their heads all the information required to analyze the symptoms and find out what is wrong with that person.

Now, having all that information doesn't necessarily make that doctor a smart person in every area of life. Emotional intelligence has been studied and measured now to the point where it is quite openly regarded as being as important, even perhaps more important than academic intelligence. Now, our doctor may know all about symptoms but may also be an emotional wreck. The same equation relates to anyone in any profession or walk of life. Psychologists, university professors, politicians, company executives, computer experts and so on. They all will have an immense knowledge of their specific fields but because of the time and effort it takes to retain all that knowledge in that specific field, there's a very good chance other areas of their life have suffered.

Even someone like a quiz champion who has an incredible amount of knowledge and information is more than likely to have no awareness of other very important areas of their life. However, we will put that quizmaster up on a pedestal simply because he has retained a lot of facts. This seems crazy to me.

In most western cultures there is a perceived cultural divide between public (government run) schools and private (non-government) schools. Again the fallacy here is that high academic achievement is everything. Some of the more "well off" people in the community will pay an enormous amount of money to put their children through a schools system where, by virtue of the money spent, the parents can demand an enormous academic focus. Therefore it is perceived that the children who go through the government run school system, which cost the parents only a fraction of the cost of private schooling, are not as bright. Fallacy.

Continued studies over more than twenty years now have proven that young people attending universities that have come through the government run school system actually fair better at those universities than the young people who've come through the private school system. So much for all the academic focus. Anyway, the point remains that an academic focus does not equate to an intelligence quota.

So, you see, knowledge and intelligence are broad and sweeping topics in our lives. We all have immense knowledge and intelligence. All of us. Just some of us have more in certain areas than others. There should be no judgment attached to that knowledge or intelligence. Just respect. A doctor needs to have respect for the knowledge a plumber has for his/her trade, and visa versa. Not one of them is "better" than the other. There has just been different kinds of retention's of knowledge that have taken place. The same can be said for a university professor and a farmer. I mean, I think I know which one would be the wiser of the two. However the professor may have some knowledge that could be helpful to the farmer. They could both help each other. Again, not one of them is better than the other. Just different. We could go on like this indefinitely but suffice to say that the bottom line is, no matter what walk of life any of us come from the only real important thing we all need to know is that we need to respect each other.

So, with that in mind, there is absolutely no reason whatsoever for anyone to feel unworthy or unintelligent because of what their occupation is. A very successful millionaire was once asked what did he need to make him happy. He answered with a list of about ten things including earning more money each year, running a marathon and so on. He wouldn't be happy until he achieved these things. Another man with a huge smile constantly on his face, and a blue-collar occupation, was asked why he was so happy all the time and he answered that every day he woke up and was on top of the ground, then he was happy.

Self-esteem is not attached to how much academic knowledge you have or by how much money you have and so on. Self-esteem is only ever attached to how you feel about yourself. If you have self-love then it doesn't matter where you are, who you are or what you're doing. With self-love you'll always be a success and you'll always be very, very smart.

AFFIRMATIONS

- ❑ I am smart and intelligent where ever I am
- ❑ I acknowledge my wisdom
- ❑ My emotional intelligence is important to me
- ❑ I'm a clear thinker
- ❑ I express my intelligence easily
- ❑ I know what I know and I know that's a lot
- ❑ I think, therefore I am, therefore I'm clever
- ❑ No one is smarter than me
- ❑ I have unlimited intelligence
- ❑ I am my own unique self, intelligent and wonderful
- ❑ Every day and in every way I'm getting smarter and smarter
- ❑ I learn something new every single day

MEDITATION

1. Identify your issues and/or problems in terms of knowledge and intelligence that you want to heal.
2. Find your quiet space and time.
3. Put on your meditation music and ask for healing from your "source" in terms of your issues and/or problems.
4. Relax, focus on your breath and allow yourself to drift away to a place of total relaxation, release and healing.

A few crystals that would be ideal to be used during this meditation or to carry around in regards to issues concerning knowledge and intelligence are:

Pyrite: (brassy, silver to gold coloured iron mineral which mostly occurs in clusters and chunks) Pyrite assists with all concentration and memory. Can also be used in combination with flourite and calcite as part of the mental trinity.

Purple Flourite: (Purple) Provides clarity and concentration. Is also excellent for students as a study aid. Especially those learning complex subjects such as science and medicine.

Gold Calcite: (Gold) Gold Calcite is good for when you need to be mentally alert. It also helps to channel the highest mental faculties and enhances clarity of thought, vision and the ability to see the truth.

Star Mica: (yellow/gold) Star Mica is excellent for developing the intellect. Academics could well use a piece in their classrooms.

Pyrite can be placed on all of the chakra points for the best results. Purple flourite Is best placed on the third eye chakra. Gold calcite is best on the solar plexus or Crown chakras and the Star mica is best on the solar plexus chakra.

VISUALIZATIONS

If you've seen yourself for a long time as a person of little knowledge then you need to take you five minutes and find a quiet place.

There you need to still the body and the mind and begin to visualize yourself as a person of knowledge. See yourself, very clearly and in the "now", using your knowledge and intellect comfortably and securely.

If you've felt nervous and unworthy around certain people in your life who you consider to be smarter than you then you need to see yourself with them right now feeling totally confident about who you are and what you know. See yourself as wise and knowledgeable due to your life experience. Know that you are as smart as them in your own way.

See yourself in all the facets of your life feeling intelligent, knowledgeable and wise in all situations because of what you've learnt in all areas of your life thus far. See yourself not feeling a lesser person because you mightn't have a tertiary degree or something. Feel safe and secure in the knowledge that you are as worthy as anyone else because of what you know.

Before enlightenment
Chopping wood
Carrying water
After enlightenment
Chopping wood
Carrying water

ZEN PROVERB

MONEY

MONEY...THE GREAT ARBITER OF SELF-LOVE, self-esteem and self-worth! Or so we have been led to believe. What is money? Why do we crave it so? Why has it become such a dominant force in our western culture? Why can't I have lots of it? Why does it always elude me? Why do a minority of people in this world have heaps of it while the majority has not much at all? Where does money come from? How do I get some?

These are, I'm sure, frequently asked questions in regards to money. I know you've asked yourself, or someone else, at least one or two of them. I know I have. It's a perplexing, fascinating and sometimes all-consuming subject matter.

In truth **money is simply freedom of choice**. The freedom to choose to do what you want to do. To have what you want to have. To go where you want to go. I think most people would say they want to have all the freedom of choice they can in their lives. In other words, they want to have all the money they can in their lives. However most people don't have that.

Why is that? Well, if you do not have a healthy dose of self-love, self-esteem or self-worth then you won't believe that you deserve to have total freedom of choice.

You will feel, deep down in your sub-conscious, that you aren't worthy of expensive, cars, houses, holidays, clothes or other assorted and extravagant material possessions. Therefore you'll never put yourself in the position to earn the amounts of money necessary to gain those possessions. In fact, wealthy possessions may not even figure in your world. You may lack self-worth to the degree that you don't feel you have the freedom of choice even in terms of being debt free. You may decide that your natural place is to always be struggling to pay the bills. To never be able to get that job that will turn the corner for you. That when money does actually come into your life you must always let it slip through your fingers without using it wisely.

As already mentioned in this book all of our actions occur because of our belief system and our belief system is rooted in our thoughts and our thoughts are a product of our conditioning. If our conditioning has been negative in terms of money then, naturally, our thoughts will be negative in terms of money. Those negative thoughts will create a negative belief system regarding money that will guarantee our actions will always keep an abundance of money safely out of our reach. To change our actions in order to create different outcomes we MUST FIRST CHANGE OUR THOUGHTS.

There are countless examples of people going to all the right seminars on wealth creation, reading all the right books on wealth creation, listening too all the right tapes and CD's and watching all the right videos and DVD's on wealth creation and not **creating** any new **wealth** whatsoever! This happens constantly. There are also statistics to prove that a vast majority of people who suddenly win millions of dollars in lotteries invariably lose all of their new found fortune in a relatively short amount of time.

All of this happens because none of these people have actually changed their negative thought patterns in terms of their wealth worthiness. If you don't believe that you deserve to have large amounts of money in your life then your actions will make sure you don't get it or keep it.

Now the next logical question here is, why do I want money? The simple answer is, "because money will make me happy". This is absolutely wrong.

MONEY WILL NOT MAKE YOU HAPPY!

In a recent interview the actor, producer and director Mel Gibson spoke of his journey in life. He mentioned how, at the pinnacle of his fame, when he was regarded as the sexiest man alive, when he was earning millions of dollars as a top line Hollywood star, when he could have, be and do anything he wanted, he was, in reality, totally miserable. He said he was miserable to the point of depression. To the point where he stood on a cliff top and contemplated throwing himself off. He created the analogy of himself standing before a form of pig's feeding trough full of absolutely everything a man in this world could want. He said he gorged himself. He ate his fill. He ate his fill over and over and it was never enough! That's an amazing lesson to learn from a man such as he. Be happy with who you are right here, right now. All the fame and fortune in the world is not going to make you happy with who you are right here, right now. Only you can do that, and you can do that by deciding that you are worthy of being happy with who you are and making sure your thoughts reflect that decision.

However you can be happy, and have money. I'm sure that now Mel Gibson has discovered the importance of self-love that he is more than happy with his wealth. I'm sure he's happy that he can provide so well for his large family, that he can make the kinds of films he wants to make regardless of the powerful Hollywood studios and that he can buy what ever he wants and travel and never, ever have to worry about a bill. That is a wonderful position to be in. You can be in a similar position but, you too, have to find your self-love. You must believe that you deserve to have wealth in your life. You must believe that you are worthy of having freedom of choice in this life. Unless you do that then no wealth generating seminar, tape, CD, book or whatever, will bring the abundance into your life that you so richly deserve.

It's up to you. If you have a healthy self-love then, as a natural consequence, you are taking full responsibility for all your own thoughts, words and actions. If you are taking full responsibility for all of your own thoughts, words and actions then you're not going to settle for anything less than complete and utter freedom of choice and, as you now know, that is what money is...freedom of choice.

AFFIRMATIONS

- ❑ I now love and enjoy financial wealth, success and security
- ❑ I am worthy of lots and lots of money
- ❑ Money now flows to me freely and easily
- ❑ I deserve millions of dollars
- ❑ Money now flows to me abundantly and perfectly
- ❑ I love money, money is good
- ❑ I deserve to have lots and lots of money
- ❑ I break the poverty cycle now
- ❑ Abundance is mine
- ❑ Money now comes to me in expected and unexpected ways
- ❑ I am a magnet for money
- ❑ I am wealthy beyond my dreams

MEDITATION

1. Identify your issues and/or problems in terms of Money that you want to heal.
2. Find your quiet space and time.
3. Put on your meditation music and ask for healing from your "source" in terms of your issues and/or problems.
4. Relax, focus on your breath and allow yourself to drift away to a place of total relaxation, release and healing.

A few crystals that would be ideal to be used during this meditation or to carry around in regard to issues concerning Money are:

Blue Aventurine: (Blue with sparkly inclusions of hematite or mica) This crystal can help with the breaking down of belief systems that prevent you from making the most beneficial decisions in regards to your abundance issues.

Citrine: (Yellow Quartz. Can range from lemon-yellow to smoky gold) Citrine raises self-esteem, optimism and personal power. It holds the energy of wealth.

Erythrite: (Brilliant pink/red mineral. Also known as cobalt bloom) Erythrite self-love and speeds up the path to self-love and self-worth. It's a no fuss stone and will enhance your ability to allow abundance to flow.

Scapolite: (Yellow, pink, violet or colourless crystal. Resembles kunzite) Scapolite works very much on an emotional level and can help with the manifestation of money in times of need.

VISUALIZATION

If you feel that you don't deserve to have an abundance of money, which basically mean's freedom of choice, then you need to change the way you feel. In order to allow abundance into your life, especially in the form of money, then you will need to visualize yourself as already having that money.

If you use affirmations and visualizations that basically ask for abundance what will happen is that you'll be perpetually stuck in that position of wanting and needing rather than having.

So what you need to do is take your five minutes of quiet time and see yourself already having the amount of money you wish to have. See yourself as having all the freedom of choice that comes with that amount. Don't allow the old negative thought patterns of unworthiness to exist any longer. See yourself as worthy of having an abundance of money in your life. See yourself thoroughly enjoying your wealth without any guilt whatsoever.

A human being
Is a single being
Unique
And unrepeatable

JOHN PAUL 11

EPILOGUE

SO HERE WE ARE, AT THE END. I really hope you got what you needed out of my book. Its all there for you if you want to use it. I just want you to feel good about yourself and if I've helped that by writing this book then I'm a happy person. Basically it comes down to the simple fact of you looking at your life and seeing if you're happy. If you're not, then take another, deeper look, find out what it is that's making you unhappy and do whatever it is you need to do to change that situation around. There is no reason to be here if we're not happy. Why live our lives in an unhappy state? We all deserve better than that. You deserve better than that. Remember it's all up to you. It's up to you to make you happy. No one else. Just you.

Use this book to help you. Use all the healing techniques and information I've given you and make yourself happy, successful and fulfilled. Put the work in. There's no greater cause in this life and on this earth than you, looking after your own well-being and finding your true self-love. I cannot stress that more. I really want to you know how important you are. I think you're important enough to write a book to help you. Surely you feel yourself important enough to do the work to make your life a better one. I hope so.

Some people think that focusing on themselves in their search for self-love is a very selfish thing to do. This is incorrect. Finding your true self-love is the most **unselfish** thing you can do. When you are in a state of self-love you can only project love. Therefore everyone around you benefit's. If you see beauty in yourself then you can't help but see beauty in everyone and everything around you. Life can do **nothing** but improve around someone in a healthy state of self-love.

So, go well. Be good. Be happy and love yourself to the best of your ability. I wish nothing but the very best for you.

Love
Paul Upchurch

SUGGESTED READING

BELOW IS A LIST OF A CHOSEN FEW of the books I've read that I suggest to you as further aids in your journey of self discovery and healing. On your journey to total and unconditional self-love. These are all fantastic authors and I think you'll find something in all of these books for yourself. Happy reading.

You Can Heal Your Life Louis L. Hay

Heal Your Body Louise L. Hay

Absolute Happiness Michael Domeyko Rowlands

Unlimited Power Anthony Robbins

Manifest Your Destiny Dr.Wayne W. Dyer

Feel The Fear, And Do It Anyway Susan Jeffers

A Guide for the Advanced Soul Susan Hayward

www.ingramcontent.com/pod-product-compliance
Ingram Content Group UK Ltd.
Pitfield, Milton Keynes, MK11 3LW, UK
UKHW040015200726
13854UKWH00001B/214